BRUCESPR

INGSTEEN

BORN TO DREAM

50 Years of the Boss

Written by

Alison James

sona
BOOKS

sona
BOOKS

First Published Danann Media Publishing Limited 2023
WARNING: For private domestic use only, any unauthorised Copying, hiring,
lending or public performance of this book is illegal.

CAT NO: SON0551

Photography courtesy of

Getty images:

Duncan1890	David Tan/Shinko Music	Bradley Kanaris
Michael Ochs Archives	Bob Riha, Jr.	Larry Busacca
Peter Cunningham/Gems/Redferns	Chip HIRES/Gamma-Rapho	Leigh Vogel/WireImage
Icon and Image	Mick Hutson/Redferns	Taylor Hill
Hulton-Deutsch Collection/Corbis	Keith Meyers/New York Times Co.	Fin Costello/Redferns
Lynn Goldsmith/Corbis/VCG	Gie Knaeps	Gary Gershoff
Will Russell	Michael Williamson/The Washington Post	Al Pereira/WireImage
Allan Tannenbaum	Frank Micelotta/ImageDirect	Brian Rasic
Tom Hill/WireImage	Kevin Mazur/WireImage	Michael Putland
Gai Terrell/Redferns	Paul Bergen/Redferns	Alexander Tamargo
Mark Weiss/WireImage	Chris Graythen	Harry Scott/Redferns
Brooks Kraft LLC/Corbis	Wally Skalij/Los Angeles Times	Sergione Infuso /Corbis

Alamy:

Landmark Media	Pictorial Press Ltd	Archivio GBB
Alessandro Bosio	United Archives GmbH	CBW
Rajko Simunovic	TCD/Prod.DB	Records
Vinyls	Michelangelo Oprandi	Sam Oaksey

Other images, Wiki Commons

Book design Darren Grice at Ctrl-d

Made in EU.
ISBN: 978-1-915343-11-6

CONTENTS

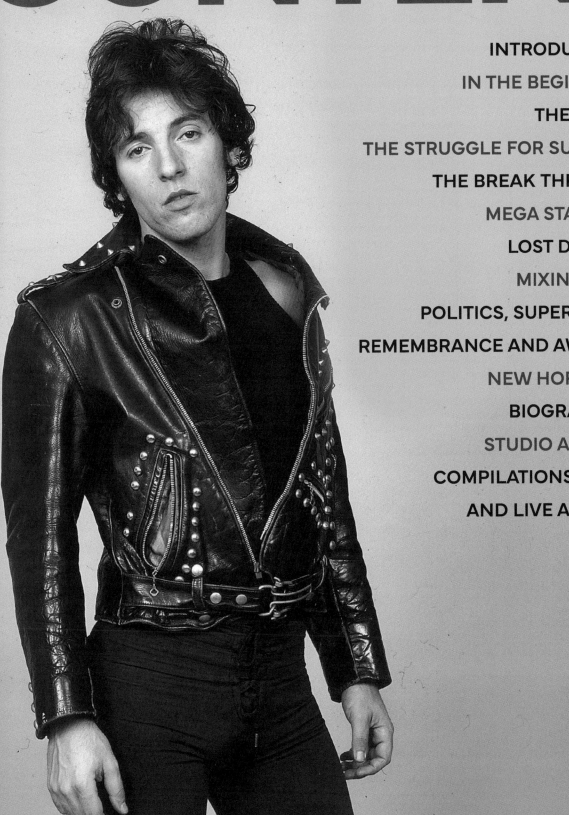

INTROD

'I spent most of my life as a musician measuring the distance between the American Dream and American reality'

Springsteen at a rally for presidential candidate Barack Obama in Nov 2008

B

ruce Springsteen. . . His career spans six decades, his cannon of work includes 21 studio albums, umpteen 'live' albums and he's performed at thousands and thousands of gigs across the globe. His music ranges from acoustic folk to R & B, soul, pop and all out rock and roll. Often described as cinematic in their scope, Springsteen's lyrics frequently explore highly personal themes such as individual commitment, dissatisfaction and dismay with life in a context of everyday situations. These themes also include social and political commentary and are rooted in the struggles faced by his own family as he was growing up in New Jersey. Widely regarded as one of the greatest songwriters of all time, Bruce Springsteen has been called a *'rock 'n' roll poet'* who *'radiates working-class authenticity'*.

This book pays homage to Springsteen's life and career – from teaching himself to play the guitar *'until my fingers screamed for mercy'* as an adolescent to becoming one of the most celebrated and influential artists in popular music history. And then there's the phenomenon that is the E Street Band – without their stalwart support over the years, the Boss just might never have made it.

UCTION

NTHEBE

'When I was growing up, there were two things that were unpopular in my house – one was me and the other was my guitar'

Bruce Springsteen

There was little in the Dutch/Italian/Irish family heritage of Bruce Frederick Joseph Springsteen to suggest that he would become one of the world's biggest, most influential rock stars. Born on September 23 1949 in Freehold, New Jersey, his father, Douglas 'Dutch' Springsteen, had problems holding down a permanent job and at various times worked as a bus driver, prison guard and mill worker - interspersed with long periods of unemployment. It fell to his mother, Adele, a legal secretary, to be the family's main breadwinner.

Raised a Catholic, Springsteen attended the St. Rose of Lima Catholic school in Freehold where he was at odds with the nuns and rebelled against the strictures imposed upon him. In third grade, a nun stuffed him in the garbage can under her desk, telling him that this was where he belonged. However, his Catholic upbringing – in addition to his working-class roots – greatly influenced the music he would go on to create. The young Bruce grew up listening to fellow New Jerseyite, Frank Sinatra, on the radio but it was watching Elvis Presley perform 'Hound Dog' on 'The Ed Sullivan Show' in 1956 that made him start dreaming of becoming a performer and musician himself. Shortly afterwards, he persuaded his mother to rent him a guitar

Bruce Springsteen when as a young man, aged 17. from the school yearbook. 1966

GINNING

from a local music store for $6 a week but his seven-year-old fingers couldn't feel their way around the fret board. Frustrated and embarrassed, he instructed her to return the instrument because there was no sense in wasting her hard-earned cash. School and academic studies continued to hold no appeal for Springsteen, then in 1964, aged 15, Springsteen heard the Beatles for the first time and it was like a bolt from the blue.

'I was in the car with my mother when "I Wanna Hold Your Hand" came on the radio,' he remembers. *'I immediately demanded that she let me out, I ran to the bowling alley. Ran to the phone booth, got in the phone booth and immediately called my girl and asked "Have you heard this band called The Beatles?" After that, it was nothing but rock 'n' roll and guitars.'*

Inspired by the Fab Four from Liverpool, he went out and bought his first acoustic guitar for $18.95, having found himself a succession of odd jobs in order to raise the funds. Over the next few months, Springsteen taught himself to play, practising over and over until *'my fingers screamed for mercy'*. He was never to be without a guitar again, spending hours in his bedroom as he attempted to master the instrument. He immersed himself in it completely, the guitar accompanying him everywhere. Friends remember him showing up at parties where there were girls, drink and drugs, only to ignore these distractions and disappear into a quiet corner with his guitar. Within six months, having beaten the acoustic *'half to death'* and with finger tips now resembling *'an armadillo's shell'*, he was ready to move up. He knew that in order to play with a band, he needed an electric guitar. Selling his pool table for $35 and with mom pitching in the same amount, he was able to purchase a sunburst, one-pick-up Kent guitar complete with small amp.

'Once home, I plugged in my new amp,' Springsteen wrote in his 2016 autobiography 'Born to Run'. *'Its tiny six-inch speaker "roared" to life. It sounded awful, distorted beyond all recognition. The amp had one control, a volume knob. It was about the size of a large bread box but I was in the game. My guitar was as cheap as they*

come but compared to the junker I'd been playing, it was a Cadillac.'

By 1965, Springsteen felt proficient enough to briefly join a teenage combo called 'The Rogues' before moving on to join the ranks of 'The Castiles', a more competent teen outfit that performed in and around the Freehold area. They wore white pants, Beatle boots, had Fab Four mop tops and performed cover songs. His passion for music eclipsed everything else, with teachers later to remark that he was *'a loner who wanted nothing more than to play guitar'*. Springsteen's audition for 'The Castiles' was so full-on that lead singer George Theiss was said to question if he was still the front man afterwards. Before long, Theiss was indeed sharing the spotlight with Springsteen, but they managed to maintain a healthy rivalry. The Castiles became popular in the area, regularly playing local gigs and even, on occasion, venturing into New York City. However, Springsteen's life at home was suffering. His father, who suffered with depression and had issues with alcohol, was highly displeased with his son's passion for making music.

'He asked me what I thought I was doing with my life,' the singer was to recall between numbers at a concert in New York City in 1976. *'We'd always end up screaming at each other. My mother would always be running in from the front room crying and trying to pull him off me, trying to keep us from fighting with each other. I'd always end up running, pulling away from him and running out the back door. Running down the driveway screaming at him, telling him it was my life and I was going to do what I wanted to do.'*

In 1967, Springsteen was seriously injured in a motorcycle accident. His leg was crushed and he sustained a concussion. Once discharged from hospital, he was laid up for several weeks at the family home. As he couldn't move, his father took the opportunity to summon a barber to cut his hair. This was the final straw for him.

'I screamed and swore at my father,' he was later to say. *'I told him I hated him.'*

These conflicts with his dad would later greatly influence Springsteen's song writing. For now, though, as soon as he was well enough to pick up his guitar, he began spending more and more time in Asbury Park, a seaside town some 15 miles east of Freehold, which had become something of a mecca for enthusiastic young musicians and bands. The Green Mermaid Café and Upstage Club, was run by Tom and Margaret Potter, a bohemian husband and wife team, who worked as hairdressers by day and created 'a scene' for musicians by night. At the Upstage, more reminiscent of a San Francisco psychedelic hang-out than mainstream shore nightclub, musicians were encouraged to '*Leave your anger and hate outside the door with your booze and drugs*'. This wasn't a problem for Bruce as he never took drugs and also barely touched alcohol at this time. The Upstage was where musicians could meet, talk about their influences and play original music. Springsteen drank it all in - writing his first songs, honing his guitar skills and taking his first steps to becoming a charismatic front man.

As pop bands gave way to more blues-based and guitar driven artists such as 'Cream' and Jimi Hendrix, 'The Castiles' – having become one of the best-known bands in the area – simply ran out of steam. Influenced by these 'heavier' bands, Springsteen formed 'Earth' – a blues/rock influenced power trio with Springsteen backed up by bassist John Graham and drummer Michael Burke whom he had met through informal jamming sessions during the spring and early summer of 1968. By now Springsteen had dropped out of college and managed to escape the Vietnam draft on account of his earlier head injury.

In early 1969, Springsteen's parents decided to head west to start a new life in California with younger daughter, Paula – their elder daughter, Virginia, pregnant with her first child, opted to stay in New Jersey with her husband. Like-wise Springsteen, relocated to Asbury Park and totally immersed himself in life there, hanging out with fellow musos including bassist Garry Tallent, organist and accordian player Danny Federici, drummer Vini Lopez and guitarist Steve Van Zandt. Springsteen didn't know it at the time but it would be these four guys who would form the nucleus of The E Street Band, mark one. . .

THEC

*'I have never been so overwhelmed
by a totally unknown talent'*

**Quote about Springsteen from journalist Philip Elwood,
music critic for the San Francisco Examiner**

B

y April '69, Springsteen had given birth to his next band,
'Child', with Lopez, Federici and bass player, Vinnie Roslin.
'Child' conducted its first rehearsal at new manager
Carl 'Tinker' West's surfboard factory in Asbury Park.
Tinker, a legendary surfboard designer/shaper with
San Diego based 'Challenger West Surfboards', had
come to the Jersey shore in 1966 to set up a 'Challenger
East' business. Plus, he was a guitarist and skilled harp
player in his own right and had also set up a concert
promotion business called 'Blah Productions'.
'Child' gigged extensively around New Jersey,
venturing further afield on occasion to Virginia.
By November '69, in order to avoid confusion with
another group by the same name, the four-piece
became 'Steel Mill'.

CLIMB

FRI. **CHILD** SEPT.
SAT. 19·20
FROM NEW JERSEY
THE CENTER
2.00 EACH   9:00 P.M.
313 NORTH LAUREL
·PLUS·IN LIVING COLOR·
AIREFLOW LIGHT SHOW

**STEEL
MILL**

MERCY
FLIGHT

MARLO MAYS
& THE
STINGERS
BLUES
BAND

HIGH ATOP RICHMOND'S
**7th & MARSHALL STS
PARKINGDECK**
AUG. 14 8:30pm $2.50..

Child & Steel Mill gig posters

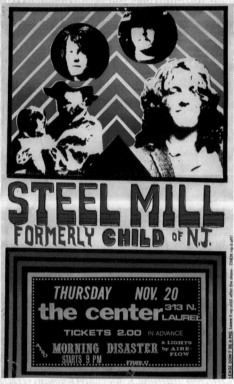

Steel Mill gig posters

After playing and touring together along the East Coast for nearly a year, 'Steel Mill' received an invitation to play at the Matrix in San Francisco. Opened in 1965 by Jefferson Airplane's Marty Balin, the Matrix was one of the venues responsible for what became known as the 'San Francisco Sound', regularly hosting the likes of bands like 'Santana', 'The Dead' and, of course, 'Airplane'. In January 1970, 'Steel Mill' were booked at the Matrix to open for Boz Scaggs, an early member of the 'Steve Miller Band', and Bay Area mainstay. But when Scaggs called in sick at the last minute, 'Steel Mill' became the only act on the bill. They delivered a monumental hour-long performance to a small but attentive audience, one of whom was journalist Philip Elwood. He was music critic for the 'San Francisco Examiner' and was blown away by the four-piece, writing *'I have never been so overwhelmed by a totally unknown talent'*.

Elwood went on to praise their *'cohesive musicality'* and, in particular, singled out Springsteen as *'a most impressive composer'*. But when a recording session – Springsteen's first – didn't exactly glean the hoped-for result, ie, a recording contract and regular gigs, the band left California.

'There were simply too many good groups around for someone to pay us to play,' Springsteen was later to write. *'We could survive as musicians only on our little sliver of the East Coast. We had to get back.'*

Shortly after returning from San Francisco, Roslin left Steel Mill or rather he was 'let go' – the other three members of the band feeling his commitment was lacking. Steve Van Zandt was drafted in to replace Roslin – Van Zandt's commitment exemplified by the guitarist immediately going out to buy a bass guitar. Carl "Tinker" West continued to guide and manage the band throughout 1970, allowing Springsteen to concentrate on his song writing. They built up a healthy following on East Coast college campuses and opened for several internationally-known acts, including Roy Orbison and Ike and Tina Turner. But by the end of the year, Springsteen was restless and wanted to change direction.

'I had stylistically outgrown Steel Mill's heavy rock, roots 'n' boogie,' he said. *'I was listening to Joe Cocker's "Mad Dogs and Englishmen" and Van Morrison, and was interested in returning to my soul roots. I talked to Mad Dog Lopez and Steve about moving forward with me into something completely different, a 10-piece horns-and-singers-augmented rock and soul band, playing nothing but new material.'*

'Steel Mill' played their final show on January 23, 1971. Over the next 18 months - as Springsteen sought to shape a unique musical and lyrical style - he performed with Lopez, Federici and Van Zandt in 'Dr. Zoom & the Sonic Boom' (early- to mid-1971), 'The Sundance Blues Band' (mid-1971), and 'The Bruce Springsteen Band' (mid-1971 to mid-1972). Around this time, Springsteen acquired his nickname of 'The Boss' due to his habit of collecting their fee after a show and then distributing it evenly among his band mates. It was also around this time that he became acquainted with 16-year-old African American keyboard virtuoso, David Sancious – a musician he described as having *'pure musical genius and incredible stage presence'* and also a gifted young sax player by the name of Clarence Clemons.

With success still eluding him, Springsteen was again beginning to reassess which direction he should go in, feeling that he should primarily hone his skills as a songwriter. Tinker was feeling

SUNSHINE IN

and GREAT BEAST present

DR. ZOOM AND THE SONIC BOOM

with BRUCE SPRINGSTEEN
and SUNNY JIM

* SPECIAL
ADDED GROUP CORNERSTONE *

** ONE BIG SHOW **
FRI. EVE. MAY 14, 8:30 PM
admission 2.50

TICKETS AVAILABLE AT

SUNSHINE IN BOX OFFICE
FIRST & KINGSLEY AVE.
ASBURY PARK N.J.
775-6876 775-6864

Tickets also available at
SOUND OF MUSIC
Monmouth Shopping Center, Eatontown - 542-4255
IGOR RECORDS
10 West Main St, Freehold - 462-9662
TURNTABLE
Brighton Ave, West End, Long Branch - 222-3010
C.J's
711 Cookman Ave, Asbury Park - 774-6814
TAPEWORM
124 Hwy 35, Neptune - 774-7705

THRIFTY THREADS
100 Hwy 36, Keyport - 739-0258
Red Bank Mall, Red Bank - 842-6145
MEN'S ROOM
Hooper Ave, Silverton - 255-1400
INNER CIRCLE
713 West Grand Ave, Rahway - 382-4441
BROADWAY MUSIC CENTER
North B'way, South Amboy - 721-7440
LYNFED THEATRE TICKET AGENCY
326 Third Street, Lakewood - 363-2601

that perhaps he'd done as much for Springsteen as he possibly could. He introduced Bruce to Mike Appel, a moderately successful guitarist and songwriter from the '50s and '60s, who had co-written several hits for 'The Partridge Family', one of the biggest pop bands of the early 1970s. It was the briefest of meetings, with Springsteen preoccupied about a forthcoming trip to California to see his folks, plus he was toying with the idea of relocating out west permanently. Once there, he changed his mind again, headed back to Jersey and gave Appel a call.

'He remembered me and told me to come on up to see him,' Springsteen wrote in 'Born to Run'. *'I went to New York City and played him my new stuff and he said these were songs we could knock down doors with. He got crazy excited as only Mike could, comparing me to Dylan, Shakespeare, James Joyce and Bozo the Clown. Mike could raise hard-ons in half a cemetery with his enthusiasm. It was what drew me to him. He could get you excited about yourself. By the time I left his office, it felt like my superstardom had been pre-ordained!'*

But before Appel took Springsteen on, he insisted that they make it legal and signed him up to a tight production contract. Springsteen was later to regret this but there was no doubt that, at the time, it was Appel's uber-enthusiasm combined with a refusal to take no for an answer that procured Springsteen a meeting with John Hammond, the legendary producer at Columbia Records who had signed Bob Dylan. Hammond later said he was so annoyed at Springsteen's now-manager's aggressive form for persistence that he was *'ready to hate Bruce'*. But instead, on hearing Springsteen play, he proclaimed that he *'had to be on Columbia Records'*.

For Springsteen, the dream was beginning to come true.

'I felt my heart rise up inside of me, mysterious particles dancing underneath my skin and faraway stars lighting up my nerve endings,' he wrote. *'We'd climbed to the heavens and spoken to the gods who told us we were spitting thunder and throwing lightening bolts. It was on. It was all on. After the years of wanting, of struggle toward that something I thought might never happen, it had happened. I was 22 years old.'*

THE STR
FOR SU

'John Hammond, Clive Davis and Columbia thought they'd signed a folk singer-songwriter. . . I convinced Mike I needed to record with a band'

Bruce Springsteen shortly before commencing work on 'Greetings from Asbury Park, New Jersey'.

H

aving met with Colombia Records' CEO Clive Davis and recorded a demo of acoustic originals for John Hammond, Bruce Springsteen signed a 10-album deal with the label on June 9 1972. But his recording advance took a while to come through and until it did, he was desperately short of money. He slept on the floor of a friend's rundown apartment during the month it took to record his first album which he would go on to name 'Greetings from Asbury Park, New Jersey'. While recording the album during the day at 914 studios situated in Blauvelt, New York state, Springsteen would then spend the evenings performing in New York City clubs.

Bruce Springsteen, circa 1972

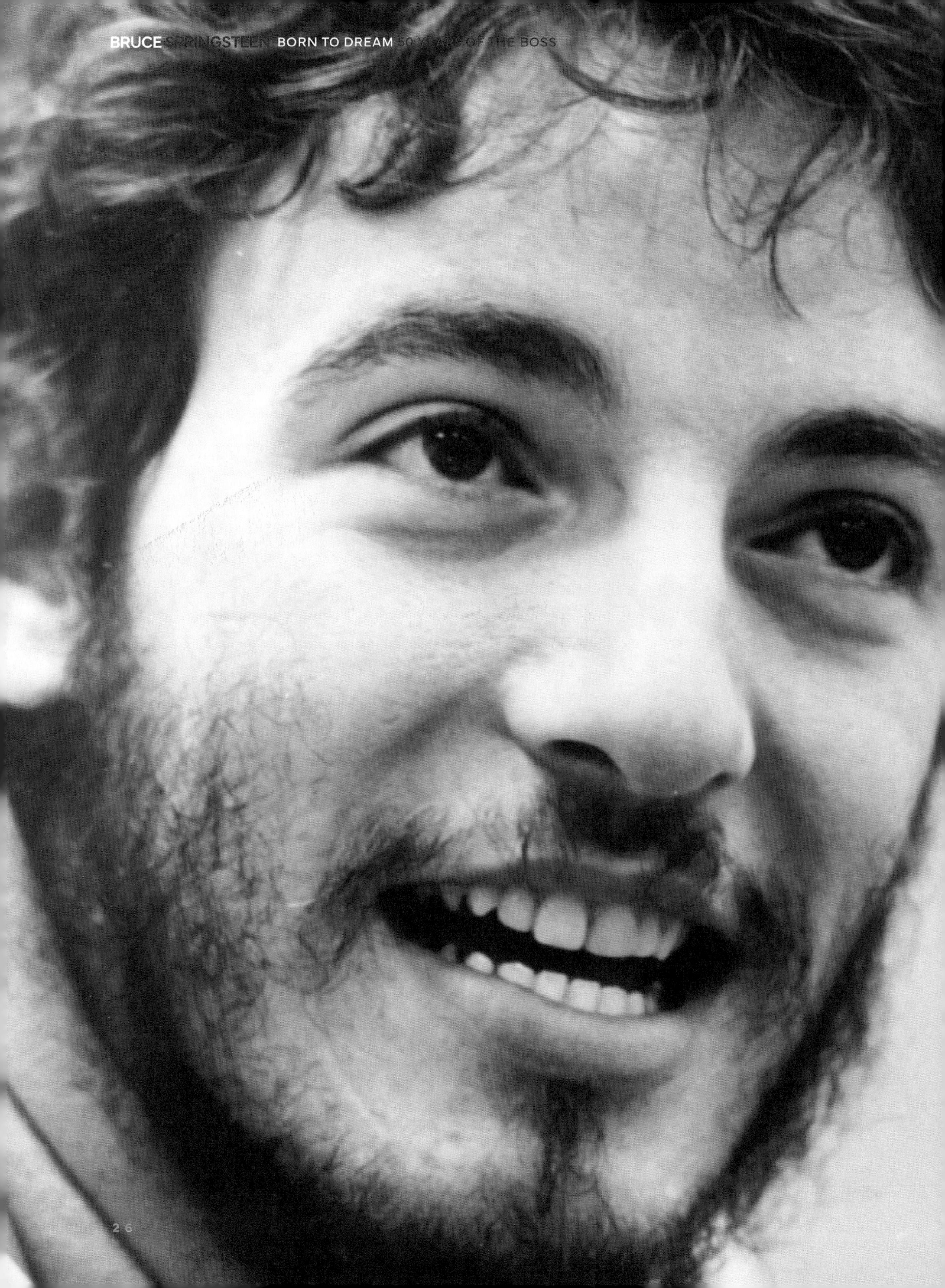

'I'd make it to the Port Authority just in time for the last bus back to Asbury,' he recalls.

The recording sessions didn't get off to the best start, with Mike Appel and co-producer Jimmy Cretecos falling out with Colombia's studio engineer. Finally, a compromise was reached and they were able to bring in their own guy, Louis Lahav, as engineer. Despite Colombia and, indeed, Appel and Cretecos expecting Springsteen to record an acoustic, solo album in the style of early Dylan, he insisted in bringing in his 'homeboys' – pre-E Street Band members Vini Lopez, David Sancious and Garry Tallent, with a cameo performance by Steve Van Zandt. The album was recorded in just three weeks.

'Most of the songs were twisted autobiographies,' Springsteen recalled. *'"Growin' Up", "Does This Bus Stop at 82nd Street?", "For You", "Lost in the Flood", and "Saint in the City" found their seed in people, places, hangouts, and incidents I'd seen and things I'd lived. I wrote impressionistically and changed names to protect the guilty. I worked to find something that was identifiably mine.'*

On the first hearing, however, Clive Davis felt there were no obvious hits and instructed Springsteen to go away and write one. He came up with 'Spirits in the Night' and also 'Blinded by the Light', featuring Clarence Clemons on sax, another future member of the E Street Band. The latter track wasn't a hit for Springsteen but four years later became a number one for Manfred Mann's Earth Band.

'I never wrote completely in that style again,' Springsteen was later to say. *'Once the record was released, I heard all the Dylan comparisons so I steered away from it.'*

'Greetings. . .' was released in January 1973. While well received on the whole by music critics, it wasn't a big seller by record company standards – shifting approximately 23,000 copies. Springsteen, however, was delighted and left wondering just who were all these strangers buying his music. Once released, 'The Boss' and his 'homies' hit the road,

Bruce Springsteen, circa 1974

opening for the likes of Chuck Berry, Jerry Lee Lewis, Brownsville Station, the Eagles and Chicago in a variety of US cities.

'Conditions were generally horrible,' Springsteen wrote. *'But compared to what? The dumpiest hotel on the road was a step-up from my home digs. I was 23 and I was making a living playing music! It's a life-giving, sweat-drenched, muscle-aching, voice-blowing, mind-clearing, exhausting, soul-invigorating, cathartic pleasure and privilege every night.'*

Springsteen halted the touring to record his second album in May 1973. 'The Wild, the Innocent & the E Street Shuffle' took three months to record. Produced again by Appel and Cretecos and recorded at 914, it was another strongly autobiographical opus with references – both lyrically and musically - to first loves, his time in 'Steel Mill', and the fun to be had hanging out with the guys. It also revealed Springsteen's growing sophistication in song structure as he switched effortlessly from rock to jazz to R n B with both Danny Federici and David Sancious back on piano to initiate the band's unique double keyboard sound. By the time the recording drew to a close, Springsteen and the band – who wouldn't officially be named as 'The E Street Band' until September 1974 – were working around the clock with Clemons and Springsteen going so far as to pitch a tent in the small studio yard, sleeping there for days while finishing their final overdubs.

As with 'Greetings. . .', critical acclaim was generally positive but this wasn't reflected in album sales. There was, however, a reason for this. Springsteen's Columbia cheerleader John Hammond had retired while Clive Davis had been fired, and artistic director Charles Koppelman was now taking charge. Having listened to the recordings, Koppelman wasn't impressed, particularly by the standard of musicianship, and requested that Springsteen re-record using 'real' musicians. Springsteen refused with the result that Koppleman refused to promote the release in any meaningful way, going so far as to instruct radio stations not to give the album airtime. The result? The album would disappear. Ditto Springsteen.

'What could I do?' Springsteen was to later recount. 'This was my band. I was committed to them. And I liked the way the recording was. When we toured to promote "The Wild, The Innocent. . . " few knew that it had even been released.'

Fortunately fate intervened – or rather the son of Irwin Siegelstein, the new CEO of Columbia. Having been to see Springsteen and his band perform and coming away impressed, Siegelstein Jnr arranged for artist and CEO to have dinner. Springsteen recalls Siegelstein saying to him, 'How can we fix this?' The executive was an honourable man and realised that Springsteen was an asset to the company.

'He wanted to put things right,' says Springsteen.

A publicity campaign was put in place with positive reviews for the album following soon after. However, it was a too little too late with the second album selling no more copies than the first.

It was while Springsteen was touring the album that problems came to a head with Vini 'Mad Dog' Lopez. He fell out with Mike Appel, had a run in with Clarence Clemons and kept getting into fights. Lopez was a loose cannon but the bottom line for Springsteen was that his music was changing and he required a drummer to reflect this.

'I needed a drummer with a more sophisticated palate,' he wrote many years later. 'With clearer and better time for the music I was now writing. I loved Vini and still do. His drumming graces my first two albums with a beautiful soul and eccentricity that perfectly fit the eclectic spirit of those songs. He was a part of the E Street Band through its toughest times, when it truly was a folk band up from the streets of Asbury Park.'

Lopez's replacement was a friend of David Sancious, known as Boom Carter. He was a jazzier drummer than Springsteen may have initially chosen and only stayed with the E Street Band long enough to record just one track on the next album. But it was this track that would change all their lives. . .

THE BREAK

'I saw the future of Rock and Roll,
and its name is Bruce Springsteen'

Jon Landau, Springsteen's future manager and producer

On the road for much of 1974, Springsteen had the tighter-than-tight, now officially-named E Street Band - with their seamless ability to switch from rock to soul and Motown through to R & B, jazz and pop on stage - to back him up and every show pulsated with excitement. Word spread of these unmissable performances and the music media flocked to witness them. One scribe was high respected wordsmith, Jon Landau, a sometime contributor to 'Rolling Stone' magazine, who saw Springsteen and the E Street Band opening for Bonnie Raitt in Massachusetts.

'I saw the future of Rock and Roll, and its name is Bruce Springsteen,' wrote Landau for 'The Real Paper'.

Columbia picked up on this and Landau's quotation was used on new publicity material for 'The Wild, the Innocent and the Wall Street Shuffle'. Sales began to pick up as Springsteen and the band continued to tour, packing out venues night after night. The tour that summer helped create a buzz around Springsteen, and in August he returned to 914 Sound Studios in Blauvelt, N.Y., to record a song which he'd written earlier in the year at his home in Long Branch, New Jersey. The song would appear on his third contractual album with Columbia Records – the album which he knew would either make him or break him.

Bruce Springsteen plays at the Trenton War Memorial, Trenton, New Jersey, November 1974

Bruce Springsteen prepares to embark on the E Street Band's "Born To Run Tour" with a 19-hour marathon rehearsal studio session on July 19, 1975, at The Record Plant in New York City.

Bruce Springsteen & Clarence Clemons at the Trenton
War Memorial, New Jersey, November 1974

'*One day I was playing my guitar on the edge of the bed, working on some song ideas,*' Springsteen wrote, '*and the words "Born to Run" came to me. I liked the phrase because it suggested a cinematic drama that I thought would work with the music that I'd been hearing in my head. I had to make a record that was the embodiment of what I'd been slowly promising I could do. It had to be something epic and extraordinary, something that hadn't quite been heard before. I wanted to deliver its message in less time and with a shorter burst of energy.*'

Springsteen consulted his new friend Jon Landau for advice. He wanted a big wall of Motown-like sound - '*Roy Orbison singing Dylan, produced by Phil Spector*', he described it as. Landau hadn't rated the sound quality of Springsteen's first two albums and suggested they move to a better recording studio. Sessions began at Manhattan's Record Plant in March 1975, with Landau installed as co-producer along with manager Mike Appel.

It took Bruce and his band months to record the title track alone, with versions including string section overdubs, a choir on the chorus and one with a double-tracked lead vocal. The sessions slogged on for hours at a time with Springsteen having difficulty communicating his vision, largely because he was unsure of what it was.

It was during a recording session of 'Tenth Avenue Freeze Out' in July 1975 that Springsteen and Landau asked a visiting Steve Van Zandt to take charge and instruct the horn players. Van Zandt duly sang each horn player their part, with the lines, the timing and the inflection all perfect. Van Zandt also helped Springsteen perfect 'Born to Run' by adding its memorable guitar line riff.

Meanwhile, Appel leaked the rough mix of the single 'Born to Run' to some radio stations. The response was enough to convince Columbia that their faith in Springsteen would finally pay off. With an astonishing nine months to go before the album saw the light of day and with no confirmed album release date, various radio stations in the US began to play 'Born to Run'. This early endorsement had two effects - when the official single did become available, it was an instant smash. And Columbia realised that their signing had the capability to create hits. Springsteen found making the album a struggle, though. A perfectionist, he was never happy with what he produced. At the end of the gruelling months of recording, even though the album was finally finished, Springsteen was miserable, later saying, *'I hated it! I couldn't stand to listen to it. I thought it was the worst piece of garbage I'd ever heard.'*

Bruce Springsteen performs with The E-Street Band at Alex Cooley's Electric Ballroom on August 22, 1975 in Atlanta, Georgia

Bruce Springsteen takes a break from the soundcheck before performing at the Alex Cooley's Electric Ballroom on August 22, 1975

Jon Landau took charge, insisting that the album – which would be named the same as the single – was released. On August 25 1975, it hit the stores and was a commercial – as well as critical - success, peaking at number three on the Billboard 200 charts and eventually selling six million copies in the United States.

'Born To Run' launched Springsteen towards mega-stardom, famously getting him on the covers of 'Time' and 'Newsweek' magazines. But almost inevitably, there was fall-out. Springsteen parted with long time manager Mike Appel and replaced him with Landau. This was to bring problems of a different kind. Appel resented the ease with which Landau and Springsteen worked with one another. Following the success of 'Born to Run', Appel suggested that he and Springsteen renegotiate their contract, but Springsteen preferred to take things on a day-to-day basis. No consensus could be reached so Springsteen felt compelled to go down the legal route. Two days after he filed a suit against Appel for fraud, undue influence and breach of trust, Appel responded by seeking a permanent injunction in New York State Supreme Court barring Springsteen and Landau from entering the recording studio together. Legally Springsteen could go on the road but was unable to go back into the studio to make a follow-up to 'Born to Run'. Back out on tour he and the E Street Band went, criss-crossing the US, Canada and Europe until well into 1977. After over a year of legal wranglings, Springsteen and Appel finally came to an agreement and officially parted ways. Appel gave up publishing rights on most of Springsteen's music in exchange for $800,000, and he took a cut in production points from six to two. Springsteen breathed a sigh of relief. Finally, he could get back into the studio.

Bruce Springsteen performing live
on the Born To Run tour c.1975

Steven Van Zandt and Bruce Springsteen being interviewed on-air by Cat Simon at WQXI Radio, March 27, 1976, Atlanta, Georgia

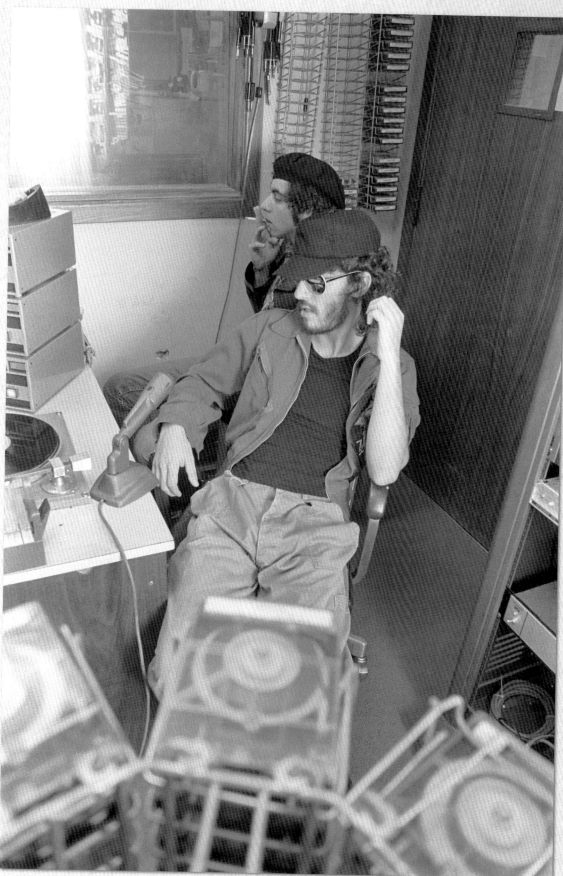

MEGA S

MEGA S

'My greatest fear was that success was going to change or diminish that part of myself'

Bruce Springsteen

I n June 1978, 'Darkness on the Edge of Town' was released. Musically, this album was a turning point in Springsteen's career. Gone were the raw, rapid-fire lyrics, outsized characters, and long, multi-part musical compositions of the first three albums. These songs were leaner, more carefully drawn and began to reflect Springsteen's growing intellectual and political awareness beyond the confines of New Jersey.

'I'd started listening to country music which I hadn't really done before,' he recalls. *'For the first time I really connected with Hank Williams. What I liked about country music tackled adult concerns.'*

Reviews were overwhelmingly positive with critics praising the maturity of the album's themes and lyrics. It remains one of Springsteen's most highly regarded records by both fans and critics and several of its songs have become staples of Springsteen's live performances. In 2020, it ranked at No. 91 on Rolling Stone's list of the 500 greatest albums of all time. The Darkness tour across the US during 1978 became legendary for the intensity and length of its shows.

Bruce Springsteen plays at the Spectrum, Philadelphia, Pennsylvania, May 26, 1978

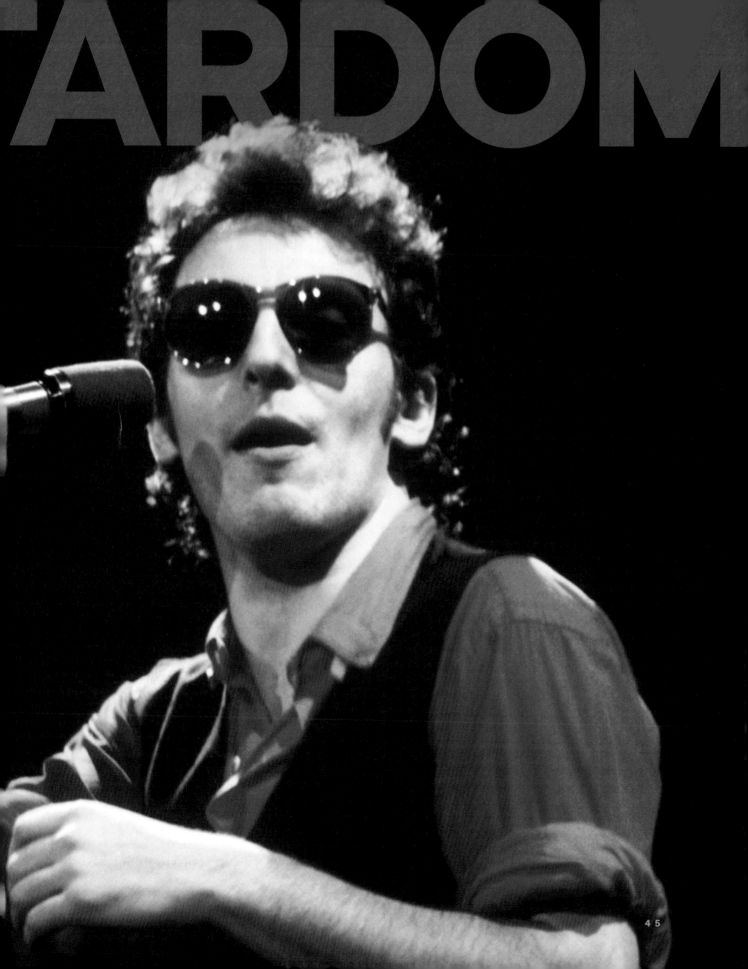

Bruce Springsteen and the E Street Band 1977

Bruce Springsteen, circa 1978

Springsteen rehearses with "Miami" Steve
Van Zandt, and the rest of the E Street Band

His next album was 'The River', released in October 1980, a sprawling double disc choc-a-bloc with radio-friendly tracks such as 'Hungry Heart' and the album's title track which had been inspired by his sister, Virginia, who had fallen pregnant as a teenager, married her high school sweetheart and missed out on a life of her own. Springsteen finally landed on number one on Billboard's Top 200 album chart, knocking Barbra Streisand's 'Guilty' off the top spot.

Before the album was released, he and the E Street Band embarked on the River tour in autumn/fall 1980. The Boss and his boys had never been so in sync.

'You hear a lot of talk about bands being family,' says drummer Max Weisberg. *'At that time, it really was that because what we had was our relationships and the music Bruce was writing.'*

Clarence Clemons, Bruce Springsteen, Garry Tallent and Miami Steve Van Zandt perform at The Spectrum on December 8, 1980 in Philadelphia, Pennsylvania

The first leg of the tour took place in arenas across the US, starting in early October 1980, and lasting through to the very end of the year. After a three-week holiday break, a second leg continued with 26 shows through early March in Canada and the U.S. The third leg of the tour, during April through to June 1981, represented Springsteen's first real foray into Western Europe - his first appearances there since his very short venture there following the release of 'Born to Run' in 1975. Thirty-song sets were often seen and shows ran up to four hours. It was during this tour that Springsteen's reputation for marathon performances really took hold. A couple of concert traditions began during this tour. Near the end of 'Sherry Darling', Springsteen would pull a young female out of the front rows and dance with her on stage. This practice would become famous when he did it in the subsequent Born in the USA tour during 'Dancing in the Dark'. When playing his new (and first) Top 10 hit, 'Hungry Heart', Springsteen let the audience sing the first verse and chorus, a ritual that would be solidified on subsequent tours as well.

'The River' was followed by the stark, solo, acoustic 'Nebraska'. While this album did not sell as well as Springsteen's three previous albums, it garnered widespread critical praise, including being named 'Album of the Year' by Rolling Stone magazine, and influenced later works by other major artists.

Springsteen is, of course, best known for his 1984 album, 'Born in the USA' which sold 15 million copies in the U.S., 30 million worldwide, and became one of the best-selling albums of all time with seven singles hitting the Top 10. The 'Born in the U.S.A.' period represented the height of Springsteen's visibility in popular culture and the broadest audience he would ever reach. From June 15 to August 10, 1985, all seven of his albums appeared in the UK Albums Chart.

Bruce Springsteen during his Born in the U.S.A. tour in Philadelphia, 19 September, 1984

Original Born in the U.S.A. poster

BORN IN THE U.S.A./BRUCE SPRINGSTEEN

Bruce Springsteen perfoming on the

Born in the USA Tour, September 1984

Bruce Springsteen and E Street Band perform during the last show of the "Born in the U.S.A. Tour", October 2, 1985, Los Angeles, California

'Born in The USA went nuclear,' Springsteen wrote in his memoirs. 'I knew I had a real runner in the title cut but I didn't expect the massive wave of response we received. It's always a bit of a mystery when something breaks that big. At 34, I decided to ride it out and enjoy it. I'd grown strong and knew how to withstand the spotlight.'

The 'Born in the USA' tour was his longest and most successful to date. It featured a physically transformed Springsteen - after two years of body-building the singer had bulked up considerably. Steven Van Zandt had decided to go solo after recording the album and was replaced by Nils Lofgren. It was also the first tour to feature Springsteen's future wife, vocalist Patti Scialfa. The tour started in June 1984, taking in the US and Canada. In March 1985 they then went to Australia, Japan and Europe. It then headed back for a second leg of the U.S. tour in which Springsteen and the E Street played to sold-out football stadiums. After 16 months on the road, the last gigs were in Los Angeles in October 1985 – the tour having grossed $80–90 million overall.

Bruce Springsteen and Patti Scialfa perform on stage at Hippodrome Vincennes, Paris, France, 19th June 1988

His private life was looking just as rosy. Having played the field with enthusiasm for 10 or so years, Springsteen had fallen in love with Hollywood actress Julianne Phillips. The two met in October 1984 and were married the following May. But within three years, the marriage was over. Springsteen's next album, 'Tunnel of Love' which was released in 1987 reflected on the breakdown of the marriage and of his failings, he felt, as a husband. Not only was his marriage coming to an end but also his ties with the E Street Band were beginning to loosen. Indeed, they only played on selected tracks on 'Tunnel of Love.' After the four-and-a-half month long 'TOL' tour, followed by the six-week, 20 date 'Human Rights Now' international tour benefitting Amnesty along with the likes of Sting and Peter Gabriel, Springsteen told the band it was time for him to move on.

'I wanted to experiment with other musicians,' he was later to reflect. *'It was painful but in truth we all needed a break. After 16 years, a reconsidering was in order. I left in search of my own life and some new creative directions.'*

LOST D

A

'The '90s were a lost period for me in terms of work. I didn't do a lot of work. Some people would say I didn't do my best work'

Bruce Springsteen

s the 1990s dawned, life was looking very different for the Boss. On a personal level, he had divorced Julianne and started a serious relationship with E Street Band vocalist, Patti Scialfa, with whom he'd fallen in love on 'The Tunnel of Love' tour. By July 1990, he'd become a father to first born Evan (two more children would follow in quick succession – Jessica born in 1991 and Samuel in 1994). In June 1991, he and Patti had married. Marriage, babies and commitment brought about distractions and it took him almost two years to record his ninth studio album, 'Human Touch'. However, but just before his marriage, Springsteen had a sudden burst of creativity and wrote and recorded what would become his 10th album, 'Lucky Town', in just three weeks. 'Human Touch' and 'Lucky Town' were released simultaneously in spring 1992.

'I realised that the two albums together kind of tell one story,' he said. *'There's "Tunnel of Love", then there's what happened in between which is "Human Touch", then there's "Lucky Town".'*

Although selling millions of copies, neither album stayed as long in the charts as his other work. And neither were they particularly well received by the critics, with some saying that success and personal contentment had made him seem *'out of touch'*

ECADE

Bruce Springsteen performing live on the Human
Touch tour, Wembley Arena, 1st July 1992

Bruce Springsteen, circa 1994

Springsteen and a new backing band set out on 'The Bruce Springsteen World Tour' from mid-1992 to mid '93, taking in the US, Canada and Western Europe. This was, of course, his first time out with another group. Looking for a different sound, he assembled an outfit that gave him both more guitar-based arrangements with a more R & B-based feel. Gone were the traditional E Street elements of organ and sax. Keyboardist Roy Bittan was the only E Street Band member retained, although Patti made a number of guest appearances. The rest of the touring band were experienced but unknown session musicians. The tour was not as commercially nor as critically successful as past tours, due to the poor reception of 'Human Touch' and 'Lucky Town'. The E Street Band were also much missed with many Springsteen fans referring to the new backing band as 'the Other Band'.

The 1990s were, as Springsteen was later to admit, his 'lost years' in terms of his work. However, he won the Oscar for his song 'Streets of Philadelphia' from the 1994 Tom Hanks' film 'Philadelphia'. His involvement in 'Philadelphia' - the story of a gay man played by Hanks who asks his lawyer to help him sue his employers who fired him after discovering he has AIDS - raised his own personal awareness of LGBT issues and reignited his political fire. In 1995, after temporarily re-organizing the E Street Band for a few new songs recorded for his first Greatest Hits album, Springsteen's political conscience provided the inspiration for his next album, 'The Ghost of Tom Joad', a mainly-acoustic work inspired by John Steinbeck's 'The Grapes of Wrath' and also 'Journey to Nowhere: The Saga of the New Under Class', a book by Pulitzer Prize-winning author Dale Maharidge. The album was generally less well-received than the similar-in-theme, 'Nebraska', due to the minimal melody, twangy vocals, and political nature of most of the songs. However, some praised it for giving voice to immigrants and others who rarely have one in American culture. On the lengthy, worldwide, small-venue solo acoustic tour to accompany the album which ran on and off from late 1995 through the middle of 1997, Springsteen presented many of his older songs – such as 'Born in the USA' - in drastically reshaped acoustic form. On occasion, he had to explicitly remind his audiences to 'shut the f**k up' and not to clap during the performance.

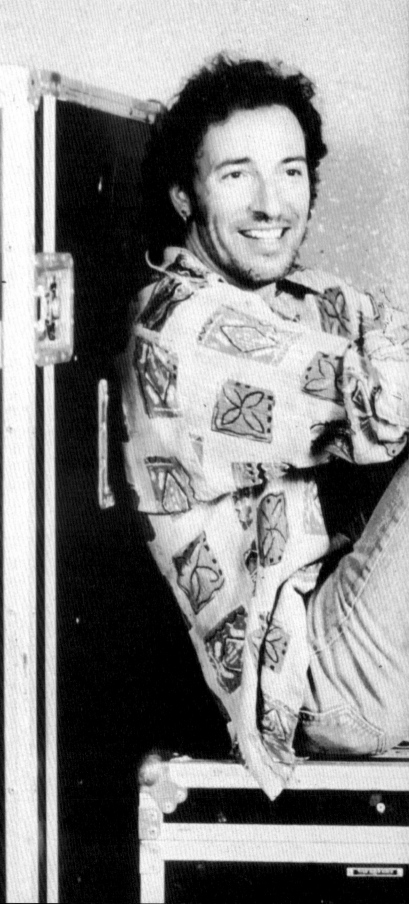

SIDE UP.

SPRING.STEEN

Springsteen sits on a trunk, backstage at the Brendan Byrne Arena, East Rutherford, New Jersey, 28th July 1992

In March 1999, Springsteen was inducted into the prestigious Rock and Roll Hall of Fame. Beforehand, Steven Van Zandt lobbied his old friend and colleague to push for the E Street Band members to be included as he felt, '*That was the legend*'. However, Springsteen, although acknowledging the part the band had played in his success, continued to see himself as a solo artist.

'I had a lot of pride about walking into John Hammond's office on my own that day in 1972,' he wrote in 'Born to Run'. *'I'd set the band aside in the early 1970s, determined to be a solo artist. My primary heroes were solo artists – Frank Sinatra, Elvis, Dylan – and I went in on my own determined to forge a solo voice.'*

While the E Street Band would not be inducted until 2014, they – in the main – supported his induction and were by his side as he received it. More importantly, the induction seemed to give Springsteen impetus to reform the band and go out on tour – although he also had misgivings. It was 10 years since they'd played together as a unit. But, according to Springsteen, when the band started rehearsing together again it could have been just 10 days before.

'On the first day of rehearsals I could feel it was all there as I kicked the band into "Prove It All Night". Ten years vanished into faint remembrance.'

The 'Reunion Tour' started on April 9 1999 and lasted over a year, with Springsteen and the E Street Band being met with a kind of *'blind hysteria'* from the audience. Originally different because of its inclusion of two keyboard instruments and a saxophone, the band was now more guitar-oriented, as different-era second guitarists Steven Van Zandt and Nils Lofgren were both included in the line-up, and

Bruce Springsteen, live at the Center for Fine Arts, Brussels, Belgium, 1st May 1996

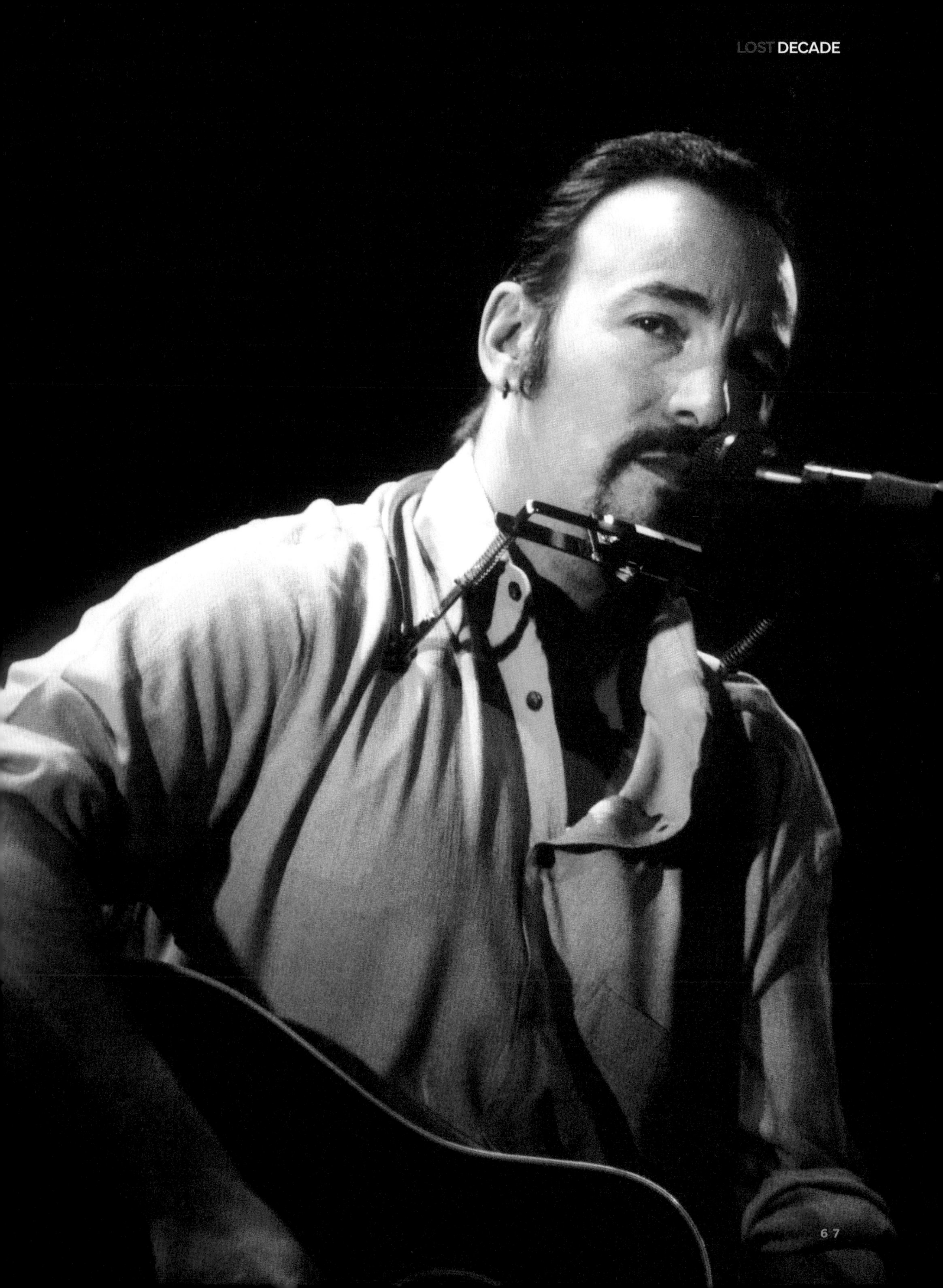

wife Patti Scialfa's greater up-front visibility added a fourth guitar. The ability of the sound system to keep the instrumental mix clear, varied from venue to venue and night to night. Highlights included a record sold-out, 15-show run at the Continental Airlines Arena in East Rutherford, New Jersey and a 10-night, sold-out engagement at New York City's Madison Square Garden. A new song, 'American Skin (41 Shots)' about the police shooting of Amadou Diallo, which was played at these shows, proved controversial.

The success of the reunion, or *'revival'* as Springsteen dubbed it, persuaded him that it was time to start writing new material for himself and the band to go into the studio with. The time was right for 'The Rising'.

E-Street band - L-R: Nils Lofgren, Bruce Springsteen, Steven Van Zandt (aka Stevie Van Zandt - Little Steven), Garry Tallent (back), performing live onstage on Reunion tour

MIXIN

*'With the correct playing style,
you can summon up an orchestra'*

Bruce Springsteen

In 2002, Springsteen released his first studio album with the full E Street Band in 18 years. 'The Rising', produced by Brendan O'Brien who had previously worked with the likes of 'The Red Hot Chilli Peppers' and 'The Black Crows', was mostly the Boss' reflection on 9/11 and was a critical and popular success – striking the right tone in its response to the terrorist attacks. Meanwhile, O'Brien brought a new freshness and focus to the band's sound and playing. The title track gained airplay in several radio formats, and the record became Springsteen's best-selling album of new material in 15 years. It was his first Number One since '95s 'Greatest Hits' and sold 525,000 copies in its first week. 'The Rising' received widespread acclaim from critics, with Rolling Stone saying it was a 'triumphant and cohesive' album that possessed a 'bold thematic concentration and penetrating emotional focus'. Uncut magazine called 'The Rising' a 'brave and beautiful album of humanity, hurt and hope from the songwriter best qualified to speak to and for his country ... A towering achievement'. At the 45th Annual Grammy Awards, 'The Rising' won the Grammy for Best Rock Album. In addition, 'The Rising' single won the Grammy for Best Rock Song and Springsteen, the Best Male Rock Vocal Performance. 'Rolling Stone' later named 'The Rising' the 35th best song of the decade while the VH1 TV channel placed it 81st on its list of the '100 Greatest Songs of the '00s'. The Rising Tour commenced in August 2002 and lasted until the following October. It was a barnstorm of an arena tour with Springsteen playing an unprecedented 10 nights in Giants Stadium in New Jersey.

GIT UP

Bruce Springsteen live, 10 August 2002

After two tours and an album with the re-united E Street Band, Springsteen decided to get back to his folky roots. The result? The 2005 solo album 'Devils and Dust', a low-key, mostly acoustic album, in the same vein as 'Nebraska' and 'The Ghost of Tom Joad'. Some of the material had been written almost 10 years earlier during, or shortly after, the Ghost of Tom Joad Tour. The title track concerned an ordinary soldier's feelings and fears during the Iraq War. The album entered the charts at No. 1 in 10 countries. Springsteen began the solo Devils & Dust Tour at the same time as the album's release, playing both small and large venues. He had considered touring with a small band line-up – thought to have been Nils Lofgren, Danny Federici, Soozie Tyrell and Steve Jordan on drums, all of whom had participated in the recording. After a week or two of rehearsals, however, Springsteen decided it was not what he wanted.

'Nils and some other folks came in for rehearsals to give me a sense of if I wanted to go with something bigger,' he said. 'But what tends to be dramatic is either the full band or you onstage by yourself. Playing alone creates a sort of drama and intimacy for the audience: They know it's just them and just you. I don't have a piano and a sax and drums behind me on this tour. So, I had to re-approach the guitar as an instrument of solo accompaniment. It becomes a bit of a new land, and I'll play it in ways I've never played it before. I'm constantly asking myself, "How can I wring as much music and meaning as possible out of those six strings?" One thing I do know - with the correct playing style, you can summon up an orchestra.'

Bruce Springsteen, Patti Scialfa, and Steven Van Zandt perform during the first show of the "Bruce Springsteen & the E Street Band" tour at the Continental Airlines Arena in East Rutherford, New Jersey, August 7, 2002

Steven Van Zandt, Dave Grohl, Tony Kanal, Pete Thomas, Bruce Springsteen and Elvis Costello perform "London Calling" in tribute to the late Joe Strummer, 23 February, 2003

Springsteen live on the We Shall Overcome tour with the Seeger Sessions band, 6th May, 2006

Springsteen's next album was a first for him. 'We Shall Overcome- The Pete Seeger Sessions', released in April 2006, was made up entirely of covers – in this instance, his interpretation of thirteen folk songs made popular by activist folk musician Pete Seeger. The seeds of the project had been planted in 1997 when he recorded 'We Shall Overcome' for the 'Where Have All the Flowers Gone: The Songs of Pete Seeger' tribute album, released in 1998. Springsteen had not known much about Seeger, given his rock and roll upbringing, and investigated the latter's music. While playing them in his house, his young daughter Jessica had said, *'Hey, that sounds like fun'* which gave Springsteen more reason to continue.

Soozie Tyrell, the violinist in the E Street Band, connected with a group of lesser-known musicians from New Jersey and New York City, and they joined Springsteen to record in an informal setting at Springsteen's Colts Neck farm. The Miami Horns and Patti Scialfa also participated. This group would become The Sessions Band. The subsequent Bruce Springsteen with the Seeger Sessions Band Tour expanded on the album's musical approach. The tour, running from April to October 2006, was billed as '*An all-new evening of gospel, folk, and blues*', otherwise seen as a form of big band folk music. The tour proved very popular in Europe, selling out everywhere and receiving some excellent reviews, but newspapers reported that a number of U.S. shows suffered from sparse attendance.

Springsteen returned to his roots for his next album, 'Magic'. Recorded with the E Street Band, it had 10 new Springsteen songs plus 'Long Walk Home', which he had performed once with the Sessions band. Springsteen allowed Brendan O'Brien (returning as producer) to pick the songs that worked the best. Recording began at Southern Tracks Recording Studio in Atlanta over a period of two months beginning in March 2007. It was complicated by the band members' schedules, and especially drummer Max Weinberg's weekday commitments to taping TV show 'Late Night with Conan O'Brien'. The band did not record as a unit – rather, during the week, Springsteen worked on vocal tracks and production, while on weekends the core band of Weinberg, Garry Tallent and Ray Bitten flew in to record the basic tracks with

Springsteen. Then, periodically, the other band members were called in as needed to overdub their parts under producer O'Brien's watch. Only saxophonist Clarence Clemons was given different treatment, with O'Brien handing the studio over to Springsteen and Clemons for the recording of sax parts due to '*a whole dynamic [between the two of them] that spans decades.'*

The album was released in September 2007, received highly positive reviews and was Springsteen's seventh number one in the UK, with first week sales of 77,692, making it his fastest-starting release of the 21st century. The album debuted at number one on the US Billboard 200 chart, selling about 335,000 copies in its first week. After falling to number two for one week, the album rose again to number one. The Magic Tour began in October 2007. In an interview at the time of the tour's announcement, Springsteen made clear that this outing would be a return to expectations after the substantial stylistic departures of the solo, multi-instrumental 2005 'Devils and Dust Tour' and the 'big folk' 'Sessions Band Tour' in 2006.

'Yeah — I'll be playing rock music this time,' he announced to many relieved and reassured fans.

But after the conclusion of the tour's first leg on November 19 2007, Danny Federici was forced to take leave of absence in order to pursue treatment for melanoma and was replaced by Charles Giordano who had played organ and keyboards on the Sessions Band Tour. Federici made his only return to the stage on March 20 2008 during the tour's third leg when he appeared for parts of a show in Indianapolis. He passed away on April 17 2008 and the next two shows of the tour were postponed as a result.

'A few weeks back we ended up onstage in Indianapolis for what would be the last time,' Springsteen eulogised at Federici's funeral. *'Before we went on, I asked him what he wanted to play and he said "Sandy". He wanted to strap on the accordion and revisit the boardwalk of our youth during the summer nights when we'd walk along the boards with all the time in the world.'*

Bruce Springsteen and The E Street Band perform at the Hartford Civic Center Coliseum at the Bruce Springsteen and The E Street Band "Magic" tour opener on October 2, 2007 in Hartford, Connecticut

POLITICS, SUPERBO AND A

'On a day like today I remember, I'm the president but he's the boss'

Barack Obama on presenting Springsteen with the Kennedy Center Honors in 2009

pringsteen supported Barack Obama's 2008 presidential campaign, giving acoustic performances throughout. Following Obama's electoral victory that November, 'The Rising' was the first song played over the loudspeakers after Obama's victory speech in Chicago. Springsteen then went on to be the musical opener at the Obama Inaugural Celebration in January 2009, performing 'The Rising' with an all-female choir before later launching into Woody Guthrie's 'This Land is Your Land' with Pete Seeger. Also in January 2009, he won the Golden Globe Award for best song from the film 'The Wrestler'. Having received a heartfelt letter from lead actor Mickey Rourke, Springsteen supplied the song for the film for free. The next month, he performed at the halftime show at the Super Bowl XLIII, having given a very rare press conference beforehand – his first in 25 years – in which he promised his set would be a '12-minute party'. It was. With the E Street Band and the Miami Horns, the set included abbreviated renditions of 'Tenth Avenue Freeze-Out', 'Born to Run', 'Working on a Dream' and 'Glory Days' – this last song complete with football references in place of the original baseball-themed lyrics. The set of appearances and promotional activities led Springsteen to say, 'This

Springsteen and the E Street Band perform at the Bridgestone halftime show during Super Bowl XLIII between the Arizona Cardinals and the Pittsburgh Steelers on February 1, 2009

Springsteen and the E Street Band perform at the Bridgestone halftime show during Super Bowl XLIII between the Arizona Cardinals and the Pittsburgh Steelers. February 1. 2009

Springsteen's 'Working on a Dream' album, dedicated to the memory of Danny Federici, was released in late January 2009. The album came out of song writing and recordings that Springsteen had continued with towards the close of recording 'Magic'. The recording of the album, again produced by Brendan O'Brien, reflected a faster pace of producing new music than Springsteen had been known for in the past.

'I hope "Working on a Dream" has caught the energy of the band fresh off the road from some of the most exciting shows we've ever done,' he said.

As with 'Magic', most of the tracks were first recorded with a core rhythm section band comprising Springsteen, Weinberg, Tallent and Bittan - with other E Street Band members' contributions added subsequently. The supporting tour ran from April 2009 until November 2009. The band performed five final shows at Giants Stadium, opening with a new song highlighting the historic stadium and Springsteen's Jersey roots, named 'Wrecking Ball'.

Springsteen received the Kennedy Centre Honors, annual honours given to those in the performing arts for their lifetime of contributions to American culture, on December 6 2009. President Obama gave a speech in which he asserted that Springsteen had incorporated the lives of regular Americans into his expansive palette of songs. Obama added that Springsteen's concerts were not just performances but *'communions'*.

'Wrecking Ball', Springsteen's 17th studio album and released in March 2012, was described by The *Hollywood Reporter* as the Boss at his *'angriest yet'*. The publication was not wrong.

'You can never go wrong pissed off in rock 'n' roll. The first half of [the album], particularly, is very angry,' Springsteen told reporters in 2012. *'The genesis of the record was after 2008, when we had the huge financial crisis in the States, and there was really no accountability for years and years. People lost their homes, and I had friends who were losing their homes, and nobody went to jail. Nobody was responsible.'*

Bruce Springsteen, at the Convention Hall in Asbury Park, New Jersey to promote his new album Working on a Dream. March, 2009

As the new album began to take shape, Springsteen mostly eschewed the E Street Band in favour of new producer Ron Aniello, who helped flesh out the songs into bigger arrangements. Aniello, who had previously worked with Patti Scialfa on her solo projects, brought some more contemporary touches such as loops and hip-hop affectations to Springsteen's classic sound, although the tracks also included country influences, Irish folk constructs, gospel tinges and bedrock arena bombast.

Springsteen and the E Street Band set out on the Wrecking Ball World Tour two weeks after the album release. It was the first tour for the E Street Band without founding member Clarence Clemons, who had died of post-stroke complications in June 2011. Fortuitously, his sax playing appeared on the 'Wrecking Ball' album – specifically on 'Land of Hope and Dreams' and the album's title track. Springsteen and the band had been knocked sideways by 'the Big Man's' sudden demise.

'Clarence doesn't leave the E Street Band when he dies. He leaves when we die,' said Springsteen as part of his eulogy.

In an attempt to fill the void left by Clemons, Springsteen added a full horn section to the E Street Band line-up for the tour, which included Jake Clemons, Clarence's nephew. Three background singers and a percussionist were also added, giving the E Street Band, at 17 members, its largest line-up ever. Patti Scialfa did not appear at all the shows due to family commitments, while Steven Van Zandt was also unable to perform on the band's Australian leg due to acting commitments. 'Rage Against the Machine' guitarist Tom Morello replaced him for those dates.

Bruce Springsteen speaks to the media during a sound-check ahead of the first show of his Wrecking Ball Tour at Brisbane Entertainment Centre on March 14, 2013 in Brisbane, Australia

During the six-month long tour, Springsteen felt inspired to start working on his 18th studio album, which eventually became 'High Hopes'. The album was recorded in 2013 during breaks in the Wrecking Ball Tour and was released in January 2014. Springsteen cited Morello, who helped re-introduce some previously recorded songs and cover songs to the recording sessions and live shows, as a huge inspiration on the album.

'The best way to describe this record,' Springsteen said, *'is that it's a bit of an anomaly but not much. I don't really work linearly like a lot of people do.'*

In April 2014, the tour was interrupted in order for the E Street Band to be inducted into the Rock and Roll Hall of Fame, 15 years after Springsteen had received the

Springsteen and the E Street Band onstage at the Rock And Roll Hall Of Fame Induction Ceremony, Barclays Center of Brooklyn, April 10, 2014

honour. He inducted both past and present members – former keyboard player David Sancious, former drummer Vini 'Mad Dog' Lopez, Garry Tallent, Max Weinberg, Roy Bittan, Steve Van Zandt , Patti Scialfa and Nils Lofgren. The late Danny Federici and Clarence Clemons were honoured for having *'provided a unique and powerful sonic template'* for Springsteen's music.

'I write to live up to the band's abilities and power onstage,' said Springsteen as he introduced them. *'That's something that's particularly significant. Even if these days, sometimes the guys are on the records, sometimes it's someone else.'*

NEW HO

'As a songwriter, a humanitarian, America's rock and roll laureate, and New Jersey's greatest ambassador, Bruce Springsteen is, quite simply, The Boss'

Springsteen being introduced before receiving the Presidential Freedom Award, 2016

T he River Tour kicked off in January 2016 in support of the release of 'The Ties That Bind: The River Collection' box set, and in celebration of the 35th anniversary of Springsteen's 1980 album, 'The River'. All first-leg shows in North America included an in-sequence performance of the entire album along with other songs from Springsteen's back catalogue. More dates were eventually announced, expanding the original three-months into a seven-month tour with shows in Europe in May 2016 and another North American leg starting in August 2016 and ending the following month. That September, saw the release of 'Chapter and Verse', a compilation album with material dating back to the 1960s. It was also marketed as a companion to his 500-page biography 'Born to Run', which swiftly became a best-seller. Two months later Springsteen was presented with the Presidential Medal of Freedom award, the USA's highest civil honour recognising *'an especially meritorious contribution to the security or national interests of the United States, world peace, cultural or other significant public or private endeavours'* from Barack Obama. Prior to receiving the award from President Obama, Bruce was introduced to the audience:

U.S. President Barack Obama awards the Presidential Medal of Freedom to Bruce Springsteen at the White House November 22, 2016

'As a songwriter, a humanitarian, America's rock and roll laureate, and New Jersey's greatest ambassador, Bruce Springsteen is, quite simply, The Boss. Through stories about ordinary people, to Vietnam veterans to steel workers, his songs capture the pain and the promise of the American experience. With his legendary E Street Band, Bruce Springsteen leaves everything on stage in epic, live, communal live performances that have rocked audiences for decades. With empathy and honesty, he holds up a mirror to who we are, as Americans chasing our dreams, and as human beings trying to do the right thing. There's a place for everyone in Bruce Springsteen's America'.

In June 2017 in another first, 'Springsteen On Broadway', an eight-week run at the Walter Kerr Theatre on Broadway in New York City was announced. The show included Springsteen reading excerpts from his autobiography and performing other spoken reminiscences. Originally scheduled to run from October 12 through to November 26, the show was extended three times - the last performance taking place on December 15 2018. For this, he was honoured with a 'Special Tony Award' at the 72nd Tony Awards in 2018. The same month, the live album 'Springsteen on Broadway' was released. The album reached the top 10 in more than 10 countries and no. 11 in the United States.

Springsteen's 19th studio album, 'Western Stars' was released in June 2019. Two months earlier, he had stated that the album was influenced by 'Southern California pop music' of the 1970s, including artists like Glen Campbell and Burt Bacharach. Upon announcing the album in April 2019, he called it 'a return to my solo recordings featuring character-driven songs and sweeping, cinematic orchestral arrangements', with a press release characterizing it as being about a 'range of American themes, of highways and desert spaces, of isolation and community and the permanence of home and hope'.

In yet another first, it was announced in July 2019, that Springsteen would premiere his film, 'Western Stars' at the Toronto Film Festival in September 2019. He co-directed the film along with long-time collaborator Thom Zimny. The film featured Springsteen performing the music from 'Western Stars' to a live audience. The film

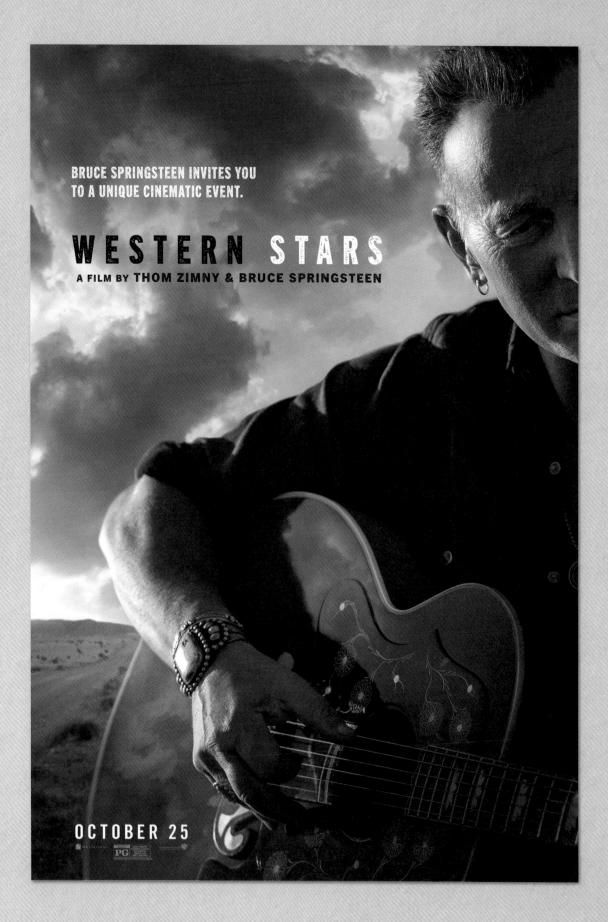

was released in cinemas in 2019, accompanied by the film's soundtrack, 'Western Stars – Songs from the Film'.

The COVID-19 pandemic didn't see Springsteen stop working. In May 2020, he appeared remotely during a livestream, no-audience concert by Celtic punk band, 'The Dropkick Murphys' in Boston. Springsteen performed their song, 'Rose Tattoo' and his own song, 'American Dream'. The event marked the first music performance without an in-person audience at a major U.S. arena, stadium or ballpark during the pandemic. During the livestream, viewers were encouraged to make charitable donations. Attracting over nine million viewers, over $700,000 was raised. He had also been busy writing a new album, his 20th studio work, called 'Letter to You' which was released in October 2020. It was Springsteen's first new studio album with the E Street Band since 2014. The themes were introspective – love, loss and the passing of time with the Boss holding a mirror up to his own mortality. The album was recorded live in the studio with no demos and only minimal overdubs (such as guitar solos, handclaps and backing vocals). It featured three tracks originally written prior to Springsteen's 1973 debut album,' Greetings from Asbury Park, N.J' – namely 'If I Was The Priest, 'Janey Needs A Shooter and 'Song for Orphans'. Springsteen had come across earlier recordings of these songs with John Hammond while assembling a compilation album. He also released a documentary entitled 'Letter to You' the same month. Shot exclusively in black and white, it was directed by Thom Zimny. To their great disappointment, Springsteen and the E Street Band were unable to tour 'Letter. . .' due to covid restrictions.

In February 2021, it was announced that Springsteen was releasing an eight-part podcast on Spotify entitled 'Renegade: Born in the USA', featuring himself in conversation with Barack Obama discussing a wide range of topics including family, race, marriage, fatherhood, the state of the U.S and the illusion of the American dream. These two giant figures subsequently had a photo-book published, the images – many of them previously unseen – accompanied by their podcast discussion put down on paper. Five months later it was announced that he would be resuming his 'Springsteen on Broadway' for a limited run at Jujamcyn's St James Theatre, beginning on June 10, 2021.

Bruce Springsteen in a scene from the promo for the
2019 ©Warner Bros film Western Stars

But what of Springsteen and the E Street Band? In December 2021, Max Weinberg indicated that he felt a tour with Springsteen and the E Street Band was looking likely before too long.

'Until the bus pulls up at my house, figuratively speaking, I'm not quite sure but I'm pretty convinced ... (that) myself, my colleagues and the people who are interested are going to be very pleasantly surprised,' he said. *'I don't make plans for Bruce Springsteen and the E Street Band but I feel very good about the next 18, 24 months.'*

Springsteen himself had very good reason to feel *'very good'*. Later that month, he sold the masters of his entire catalogue and the coinciding music publishing rights to Sony Music for a whopping $500 million. This topped the amounts both Bob Dylan and Taylor Swift had received for their canons of work by $200 million. This sale, along with his Broadway shows and projects with Obama, helped him top the 'Rolling Stone' list of the highest-paid musicians of 2021.

In May 2022, Weinberg's prediction came true when it was announced that, in February 2023, Springsteen and the E Street Band would be launching an international tour - their first since 2017 – taking in two US legs and one European.

'After six years, I'm looking forward to seeing our great and loyal fans next year,' he proclaimed. *'And I'm looking forward to once again sharing the stage with the legendary E Street Band. See you out there, next year — and beyond. . .'*

At 73, an age when many are considering slowing down, the Boss and his band are back up and rocking – and better than ever. . .

Bruce Springsteen performs during reopening night of "Springsteen on Broadway" for a full-capacity, vaccinated audience at St. James Theatre on June 26, 2021 in New York City

TBIOGS

Garry Wayne Tallent

Born:

October 27 1949

Place of birth:

Detroit, Michigan, USA

Musical background:

Took up the tuba before switching to bass guitar as a teenager. Influenced by Paul McCartney, Bill Wyman and Motown bassist James Jamerson. He joined the E Street Band in 1972, having previously played bass for several groups including Little Melvin & the Invaders, Glory Road and the Jaywalkers.

Played on:

Every Springsteen/E Street Band album, including one track on 'Tunnel of Love'.

Left The E Street Band:

When Springsteen disbanded the combo in the late 80s. Rejoined for the Greatest Hits album in 1995, and again when the Boss reformed the band four years later.

Where is he now?

Still playing/recording with Springsteen plus he has released two solo albums, recorded with, toured and produced for other artists such as Jim Lauderdale, Kevin Gordon and Steve Foubert, Bass guitarist on 2023 Springsteen and The E Street Band world tour.

Clarence Anicholas Clemons Jr. aka The Big Man

Born.

January 11 1947

Place of birth.

Norfolk County, Virginia, USA

Musical background:

Grew up listening to gospel music, aged nine he was given an alto saxophone as a Christmas present. He later switched to baritone saxophone and tenor sax. Clemons joined his first band, the Vibratones, which played James Brown covers and stayed together from 1961 to 1965. At 18 he took part in recording sessions with Tyrone Ashley's Funky Music Machine, another New Jersey band. He also performed with Daniel Petraitis, a New Jersey and Nashville legend. On seeing Springsteen and his band perform in Asbury Park one September night in 1971, Clemons asked to join.

Played on.

Every Springsteen/E Street Band album, including backing vocals on one track on 1987's 'Tunnel of Love', until his death in 2011. Appears posthumously on 'Wrecking Ball' and 'High Hopes'. Also worked with Ringo Starr, Aretha Franklin and Jackson Browne, and released several solo albums.

Left The E Street Band:

When Springsteen disbanded the combo in 1989. Rejoined for the Greatest Hits album in 1995, and again when 'The Boss' reformed the band four years later.

Where is he now?

Clarence died on June 18, 2011, following complications from a massive stroke suffered just six days before. In his eulogy, Bruce asked, 'How big was the Big Man? Too big to die.'

Daniel Paul Federici, aka Phantom Danny

Born:

January 11 1947

Place of birth:

Flemington, New Jersey, USA

Musical background:

Started playing accordion when he was seven years old, which he learned from watching The Lawrence Welk Show on TV. Having mastered classical music and the polka, his mother booked him to play at parties, clubs and on radio. While he continued his studies in classical accordion, he gained an interest in jazz and blues. Bruce and Danny met in 1968 and, together with Vini 'Mad Dog' Lopez, formed the band 'Child'. Danny would subsequently remain with Bruce through all of the Boss' early bands: Steel Mill, Dr. Zoom and the Sonic Boom, the Bruce Springsteen Band and, finally, the E Street Band.

Played on:

Did not play on Springsteen's debut album, 'Greetings from Asbury Park, N.J.' but every Springsteen/E Street Band release until ill health forced him to quit in 2007. Also played on Springsteen's solo albums 'Tunnel of Love', and 'The Ghost of Tom Joad'. Posthumously appeared on 'High Hopes'. Over the years he recorded sessions for Nils Lofgren, Joan Armatrading, Garland Jeffreys, Graham Parker and Little Steven and the Disciples of Soul.

Left The E Street Band:

When Springsteen disbanded the combo in 1989. Rejoined for the Greatest Hits album in 1995, and again when 'The Boss' reformed the band four years later.

Where is he now?

Passed away in April 2008 from skin cancer. Springsteen called him 'one of the pillars of our sound - he was the most wonderfully fluid keyboard player and a pure, natural musician.'

Vincent Lopez, aka Mad Dog

Born:

January 22 1949

Place of birth:

Neptune Township, New Jersey, USA

Musical background:

Taught himself the drums as a teenager. After graduating high school in 1967, worked in boatyards while performing in local nightclubs. Early one morning in 1969 at the Upstage Club in Asbury Park, he and his friend Danny Federeci saw Bruce Springsteen onstage. Formed the band Child with Federici and Springsteen. Mad Dog remained with Bruce during the Steel Mill, Dr. Zoom and the Sonic Boom, the Bruce Springsteen Band years. Joined the E Street Band.

Played on:

'Greetings from Asbury Park, NJ' and 'The Wild, the Innocent and the E Street Shuffle'.

Left The E Street Band:

In 1974 when Springsteen fired him for run-ins with producer Mike Appel and also coming to blows with Steve Appel, Mike's brother and the band's road manager.

Where is he now?

After leaving the E Street Band, he played drums with numerous Jersey Shore bands, including The Lord Gunner Group. Since 2004, he has led his own group, Steel Mill Retro, who have performed and recorded original Springsteen songs from the Steel Mill era. Away from his music career, Lopez has worked as a golf caddy. In 2014, Lopez was inducted into the Rock and Roll Hall of Fame as a member of the E Street Band.

David Sancious

Born:

November 30 1953

Place of birth:

Asbury Park, New Jersey, USA

Musical background:

Sancious began to learn classical piano at seven and by 11, had taught himself guitar. He was only in his teens when he first became involved in the Asbury Park music scene. In the late 1960s and early 1970s he played in various bands that included Springsteen and future members of The E Street Band, Glory Road, Dr. Zoom & The Sonic Boom, The Sundance Blues Band, Southside Johnny and Bill Chinnock. Sancious is a multi-instrumentalist but is best known as a keyboard player and guitarist.

Played on:

The first three Springsteen albums, also Human Touch (1992), Tracks (1998) and Western Star (2019).

Left The E Street Band:

In 1974 to form his own band, 'Tone'. They released several albums. Sancious subsequently became a popular session and touring musician, most notably for Stanley Clarke, Narada Michael Walden, Zucchero Fornaciari, Eric Clapton, Peter Gabriel, Jack Bruce, and Sting among many others.

Where is he now?

Sancious was inducted into the Rock and Roll Hall of Fame as a member of the E Street Band in April 2014. He continues to make solo albums and, post COVID, is hopeful of touring again.

Ernest 'Boom' Carter

Born:

September 7 1952

Place of birth:

Asbury Park, New Jersey, USA

Musical background:

As a teenager, learned to be an accomplished drummer. A childhood friend of David Sancious, in the early 1970s he worked as a session musician at Alpha Studios in Richmond, Virginia. Carter moved to Atlanta, Georgia and toured with Little Royal & The Swing Masters, a James Brown-influenced band. In February 1974, when Vini Lopez left the E Street Band, David Sancious helped recruit Carter as his replacement.

Played on:

Born to Run – his only appearance on a Springsteen album.

Left The E Street Band:

In August 1974 in order to form 'Tone' with Sancious.

Where is he now?

Although best known as a drummer, Carter is also a guitarist, keyboardist and vocalist and in 2001 he released a solo album, 'Temple of Boom', singing and playing all of the instruments. Believed to still be working as a musician.

Roy J. Bittan, aka The Professor

Born:

July 2 1949

Place of birth:

Queens, New York, USA

Musical background:

A classically-trained pianist, Bittan had been playing in Broadway musicals when he joined The E Street Band in 1974. Dubbed 'The Professor' by Springsteen because of his college education.

Played on:

Beginning with 'Born to Run' in 1975, Bittan performed on every Springsteen/E Street Band album until the group was put on hiatus from the late 1980s until reforming for 'The Greatest Hits' opus in 1995. He is the only member of the E Street Band to have co-written songs with Springsteen, with 'Roll of the Dice' and 'Real World' from 'Human Touch' to his credit, and also the outtake 'Trouble in Paradise' which was eventually released on 'Tracks'. Bittan's contributions to these songs have been credited by Springsteen as helping him break a period of writer's block experienced in late 1989.

Left The E Street Band:

Never really has. When Bruce split from the E Street Band and went on tour in 1992-93, it was with a completely new set of musicians - with one exception, Roy Bittan.

Where is he now?

Remains a valued member of the E Street Band. Between E Street tours and albums, has become an in-demand session player, playing and touring with artists from Dire Straits and Bob Seger to Lucinda Williams and Stevie Nicks. He released his first solo album, 'Out of the Box', in 2014. Playing piano and synthesiser on 2023 Springsteen and The E Street Band world tour.

Max Weinberg

Born:

April 13 1951

Place of birth:

Newark, New Jersey, USA

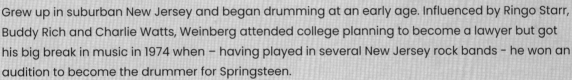

Musical background:

Grew up in suburban New Jersey and began drumming at an early age. Influenced by Ringo Starr, Buddy Rich and Charlie Watts, Weinberg attended college planning to become a lawyer but got his big break in music in 1974 when – having played in several New Jersey rock bands - he won an audition to become the drummer for Springsteen.

Played on:

The Springsteen/E Steet Band albums, minus 'Nebraska', from 'Born to Run' until the E Street Band disbanded in the late '80s. Played on 'Tunnel of Love'. Springsteen/E Street Band albums from 1995's 'Greatest Hits' onwards.

Left The E Street Band:

When Springsteen formally disbanded the combo in 1989, after which Weinberg briefly considered taking up a career in law. In 1993, Weinberg got the role as bandleader of 'The Max Weinberg 7' for TV show 'Late Night with Conan O'Brien'. Rejoined in 1995 for The Greatest Hits album and then again in '99, having worked out a plan whereby he could play with both Springsteen and O'Brien.

Where is he now?

The father of Slipknot's Jay Weinberg, Max has continued playing with Springsteen. Drummer on the 2023 Springsteen and The E Street Band world tour.

Steven Van Zandt

Born:

November 22 1950

Place of birth:

Boston, Massachusetts, USA

Musical background:

Steven learned how to play the guitar as a teenager in the mid-sixties. Grew up in the Jersey Shore music environment and was a friend of Bruce Springsteen. By the early 1970s, he was playing guitar in some of Springsteen's embryonic bands. Joined the E Street Band in 1975, after he and his soul-music expertise were called in to give a little love to the horn arrangements on 'Tenth Avenue Freeze-Out'.

Played on:

Springsteen/E Street Band studio albums from 'Born to Run' to 'Born in the USA'; Springsteen/E Street Band studio albums from 1995's 'Greatest Hits' onwards.

Left The E Street Band:

In 1984 - Springsteen is said to have written 'Bobby Jean' as a farewell. Departed in order to invest himself more in solo recording, producing, and political activism as 'Little Steven', launching, amongst other things, the 'Artists United Against Apartheid' project in 1985. He also became an actor, starring in 'The Sopranos'. Returned to the E Street Band for their 1995 and 1999 reunions and onwards, sharing guitar duties with Nils Lofgren, who took his place prior to the 1984-'85 World Tour.

Where is he now?

Has continued playing with Springsteen. Guitarist and vocals on the 2023 Springsteen and E Street Band world tour.

Nils Lofgren

Born:

June 21 1951

Place of birth:

Chicago, Illinois, USA

Musical background:

Lofgren's first instrument was the accordian, beginning at age five, which he studied seriously for 10 years. After studying jazz and classical music throughout his youth, Lofgren switched his emphasis to rock music, and focused on piano and guitar. He turned professional aged 17 and joined Neil Young's band a year later. Played piano, guitar and sang on the acclaimed platinum album 'After the Gold Rush'. Began recording as a solo artist in 1975. Nine years later, joined The E Street Band, taking over from the departing Steven Van Zandt.

Played on:

The Tunnel of Love album, all Bruce Springsteen/E Street releases from '95's 'Greatest Hits' onwards.

Left The E Street Band:

When Springsteen disbanded the group in 1989. Continued as a solo artist, also played with Ringo Starr's All Starr Band, Neil Young and other prominent musicians. When the E Street Band reconvened in 1999, Springsteen diplomatically answered the question of which guitarist would be brought back into the fold by including both Van Zandt and Lofgren.

Where is he now?

Has continued playing with Springsteen. Guitarist and vocals on the 2023 Springsteen and E Street Band world tour. Still releasing solo albums between E Street Band recording and tour commitments.

Vivienne Patricia Scialfa, aka Patti

Born:

July 1953

Place of birth:

Deal, New Jersey, USA

Musical background:

Scialfa began writing songs at an early age. Following high school, began working as a back-up singer for New Jersey bar bands. Became well-known as a vocalist on the Jersey Shore music scene. In the early '80s, Patti toured with 'Southside Johnny and the Asbury Jukes' and she worked with 'Tone', the band David Sancious formed after leaving the E Street Band. Six days before the 'Born in the USA' tour started, Springsteen – whom she'd known for years - hired her as a vocalist for the E Street Band.

Played on:

Scialfa has provided backing vocals on Springsteen's solo outings in addition to the E Street collaborations.

Left The E Street Band:

When Springsteen disbanded them in 1989 but, having fallen in love with the Boss while on the Tunnel of Love tour in 1988, they married in 1991. She and Springsteen have three children born between 1990 and 1994.

Where is she now?

Still married to Springsteen and still a member of the E Street Band. Has also recorded and toured as a solo artist. Vocalist on the 2023 Springsteen and E Street Band world tour.

ADDITIONAL MUSICIANS

Soozie Tyrell

Born:

May 4 1957

Place of birth:

Pisa, Italy

Musical background:

Born into a military family, Tyrell crisscrossed the globe as a youngster, investing herself in music before eventually settling in New York City. Her first spin in the E Street orbit came when she formed the group 'Trickster' with Lisa Lowell and Patti Scialfa.

Played on:

Tyrell's first appearance on a Springsteen album came with 'Lucky Town', where she contributed backing vocals, and since then she has appeared on every Springsteen studio album — including the non-E Street records. Tyrell and her violin were also part of the 'Seeger Sessions' album and tour band in 2006, making her one of a few E Street residents to appear in both bands.

Left The E Street Band:

Never has but then neither has she ever officially joined.

Where is she now?

Playing the violin and singing backing vocals for Springsteen and the E Street Band on the 2023 World Tour.

Charles Giordano

Born.

October 13 1954

Place of birth.

Brooklyn, New York

Musical background:

Keyboard player, organist and accordionist Charles Giordano already had a long resume prior to his work with Bruce Springsteen. He toured with Hall & Oates and Joe Cocker, and in the 1980s he was a member of Pat Benatar's regular backing band, playing on five of her albums.

Played on.

Every Springsteen/E Street band release since 'Working on a Dream'. When Danny Federici's illness at the end of the first leg of the "Magic" tour in 2007 prevented him from performing on the European leg, it was announced that Giordano, whom Springsteen had worked with previously on 'We Shall Overcome: the Seeger Sessions', would join the tour. After Federici's passing, Giordano has simply continued to hold down the spot in the band although no formal announcement has ever been made.

Where is he now?

Playing with Springsteen and the E Street Band on their world tour 2023.

Jake Clemons

Born:

February 27 1980

Place of birth:

South Carolina, USA

Musical background:

Nephew of the late Clarence Clemons. Growing up as the son of a Marine Corps band director, he attended the Virginia Governor's School for the Arts to study jazz performance and has since used those skills alongside a variety of artists ranging from The Israelites to The Swell Season. Following his uncle's passing, Jake joined the E Street Band as sax player for the Wrecking Ball Tour in 2012. He plays tenor and baritone saxophone, backing vocals and percussion but is also skilled at the piano, flute, clarinet, bass, drums, and guitar.

Played on:

'High Hopes', 'Letter to You'.

Where is he now?

Performing with Bruce Springsteen and the E Street Band on their world tour 2023. Jake also writes music and fronts his own band, 'Jake Clemons'.

STUDIO

Greetings From Asbury Park, N.J. **1973**

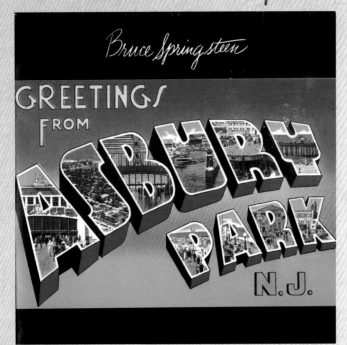

PRODUCER:	Mike Appel and Jim Cretecos
RECORDED:	914 Sound Recording Studios
	Blauvelt, New York
UK:	Did not chart in 1973 but reached 41 in 1985
	in the wake of 'Born in the USA'
USA:	60

SIDE ONE
1. Blinded by the Light
2. Growin' Up
3. Mary Queen of Arkansas
4. Does This Bus Stop at 82nd Street?
5. Lost in the Flood

SIDE TWO
1. The Angel
2. For You
3. Spirit in the Night
4. It's Hard to be a Saint in the City

Although featuring musicians Springsteen regularly played with and who would later become members of the E Street Band, his first studio album was considered a solo project. The nine songs – alive with vivid, passionate lyrics teaming with imagery and metaphor – were originally supposed to number seven but on hearing an early cut, Columbia boss Clive Davis felt there was no obvious hit and demanded that Springsteen write one! The Van Morrison inspired 'Blinded by the Light' was the result and although Springsteen didn't strike gold with it, English group Manfred Mann's Earth Band later did. Morrison's influence is also present in 'Growin' Up', 'For You', 'It's Hard to be a Saint in the City', and 'Does This Bus Stop at 82nd Street?' The album conveys Springsteen's excited energy at finally getting to record his own compositions, after years of plying and honing his craft. The New Jersey boy mixes it up – with a soulful groove being present on 'Spirit in the Night' while he channels his inner Leonard Cohen in 'Lost in the Flood', a song about Vietnam vets. Reviewers likened this new kid on the block to a new Dylan.

Although 'Greetings' didn't sell particularly well, it still holds up and is something of a vinyl love letter to the era in which it was made. Little wonder then that in 2003, the album was ranked number 379 on 'Rolling Stone' magazine's list of the 500 greatest albums of all time plus it was ranked 37th on their list of greatest debut albums.

ALBUMS

The Wild, The Innocent & The E Street Shuffle 1973

PRODUCER: Mike Appel and Jim Cretecos
RECORDED: 914 Sound Recording Studios,
Blauvelt, New York

UK: Did not chart in 1973 but reached 33 in 1985
in the wake of 'Born in the USA'

USA: 59

SIDE ONE
1. The E Street Shuffle
2. 4th of July, Asbury Park (Sandy)
3. Kitty's Back
4. Wild Billy's Circus Story

SIDE TWO
1. Incident on 57th Street
2. Rosalita (Come Out Tonight)
3. New York City Serenade

Springsteen and the now officially named E Street Band recorded 'The Wild, The Innocent and The E Street Shuffle' from May to September 1973. On this second album, 'The Boss' expanded the folk-rock approach of 'Greetings' – released only eight months previously - to strains of jazz, raunchy jazz, a kind of funk-rock hybrid and slow electric blues. Keyboard player David Sancious, whose E Street home address had given Springsteen's back-up band and the album's first track its name, played a pivotal role in this. This album was, once again, an homage to Springsteen's life thus far – the songs containing the best realization of his poetic vision which would all too soon become disillusioned. Each track tells a different story and has a different vibe – 'Kitty's Back' combines slow, electric blues with soul elements, leading into 'Wild Billy's Circus Story' – a song inspired by the circus that visited Freehold every summer. The theme of organ-driven 'Incident on 57th Street' is redemption' – a subject Springsteen would return to again and again. Then comes 'Rosalita (Come out tonight)' – a rollicking, feel-good rock n roll song with a sax solo to die for. The mood changes yet again with the plaintive piano, strings and vocals of 'New York Serenade' - a disjointed tale of life in New York City - the 'serenade' coming from the street musician playing the vibraphone. 'The East Street Shuffle' - filled with iconic characters, hoodlums, fortune tellers, and sprawling narratives that fall somewhere between historical fact and tall tale -is nothing less than the sound of summer on the Jersey coast boardwalk. As for the epic 'New York City Serenade'? Springsteen was later to say that it would never have existed if not for Van Morrison's album 'Astral Weeks'.

Born To Run 1975

PRODUCER: Bruce Springsteen, Mike Appel, Jon Landau

RECORDED: 914 Sound Recording Studios, Blauvelt, New York; The Record Plant, New York City

UK: 17

USA: 3

SIDE ONE	SIDE TWO
1. Thunder Road	1. Born to Run
2. Tenth Avenue Freeze-Out	2. She's the One
3. Night	3. Meeting Across the River
4. Backstreets	4. Jungleland

Over a year in the making, 'Born to Run' was the album that jettisoned Bruce Springsteen to rock stardom. It wasn't an easy gestation – far from it. With two ambitious but under-selling albums behind him, Springsteen desperately needed a hit for his third. With BTR he achieved this – and then some. It is a giant of an album - fuelled by tangible energy, the idealized notion of escape, and the romance of youth. With its Phil Spectresque 'Wall of Sound' production, it scorched earth upon release and remains a career-defining classic. The full-bodied 'Thunder Road' opens the proceedings. An up-lifting ode to escape with its twin guitar and sax solo twinned with lyrics *'The screen door slams, Mary's dress sways, Like a vision she dances across the porch as the radio plays, Roy Orbison singing for the lonely',* Springsteen was to later describe the song as being an invitation to the exhilarating ride that he wanted 'Born to Run' to be. 'Night' and 'She's the One' have a similar, guitar-heavy feel which, when combined with Clemons' sax gives off that distinctive E Street Band sound. An almost operatically-voiced, Orbisonesque Springsteen plays around with different textures in the strings-and-piano driven 'Tenth Avenue Freeze-Out', although not to such an extent on the album's other two ballads, 'Back Streets' and 'Meeting Across the

River'. 'Jungleland', a kind of long, urban poem in which Springsteen describes several characters who are drawn to the city's bright lights, opens with a magical 30 second intro combining violin and piano before being joined by further strings and subtle bass. The song climaxes at six minutes in before a quieter outro. Then there's the album's title track. . .arguably Springsteen's most memorable composition and biggest hit. Guitarist Steven Van Zandt helped Springsteen come up with the six-note riff that immediately hooks the listener and anchors this classic song about love, desperation and the tarnished reality of the American Dream. It has everything – tight, driving rhythm section, soaring sax, double keyboards. . . a barrage of instruments in perfect harmony, accompanied by Springsteen's yearning, heartfelt, passionate vocal. Little wonder that the 'Born to Run' album went on to sell six million copies after its release, reaching number three on the US album charts. With his third album, Bruce Springsteen had finally arrived.

*Born to Run: 30th Anniversary Edition, released 2005

This three-disc box features a sterling remaster and includes footage of Springsteen's first full-length concert DVD, filmed in London at the height of '70s Bruce-mania.

Darkness on the Edge of Town 1978

PRODUCER: Bruce Springsteen and Jon Landau

RECORDED: Atlantic Studios and The Record Plant, New York City

UK: 14

USA: 5

SIDE ONE	SIDE TWO
1. Badlands	1. The Promised Land
2. Adam Raised a Cain	2. Factory
3. Something in the Night	3. Streets of Fire
4. Candy's Room	4. Prove It All Night
5. Racing in the Street	5. Darkness on the Edge of Town

Springsteen was subdued and somewhat jaded following the lengthy legal battle with Mike Appel with the result that the introverted and pensive 'Darkness' is the antithesis of 'Born to Run'. If 'Born to Run' is epic cinema, 'Darkness' is brutal reality, its characters not dreaming of idealized escape as much as struggling against their circumstances. This is Springsteen at his poetic best. Gone are the rapid fire and lyrically dense early songs like 'Blinded by the Light', 'Growing Up' and 'Thunder Road'. On 'Darkness', the songs are shorter with not a word wasted. The stories told are darker and simpler in construction – in title track 'Darkness on the Edge of Town', 'Adam Raised a Cain' and 'Racing in the Street', we are given snapshots that express the themes and desires of entire lives. The music is almost secondary. Almost. On this album, the E Street band live up to their billing as *'one of the finest Rock & Roll groups ever assembled'* with them working collectively to support the undying energy in the songs, yet they do so without overproduction or expansiveness. Weinberg and Tallent become prominent, Van Zandt and Springsteen's guitars becomes edgily aggressive, Bittan and Federici's lines become less complex while Clemons' sax is used sparingly and powerfully. In songs like 'Badlands', the power comes from a fast-moving energy to the backing, while in other pieces like 'Streets of Fire', it emerges through the Boss' eclectic guitar. There's incredible energy and emotion in his vocals. The album provides insights on family, faith, abandonment, lies and despair. But there's hope, too. *'Make your dreams a reality'* – is the underlying message. The aim is trying to improve life even if you have nothing – this is illustrated most clearly in 'The Promised Land', 'Badlands' and the title track. Although released to mixed reviews in 1978, 'Darkness on the Edge of Town' is now widely regarded as a classic.

The Promise: The Darkness on the Edge of Town Story (2010)

Three years elapsed between 'Born to Run' and 'Darkness', and they were astonishingly prolific. This six-disc box set contains the remastered CD and 22 additional tracks, a 1978 concert DVD, a feature-length documentary, and a newly filmed E Street Band performance of the album, illuminating one of Springsteen's most richly rewarding periods.

The River 1980

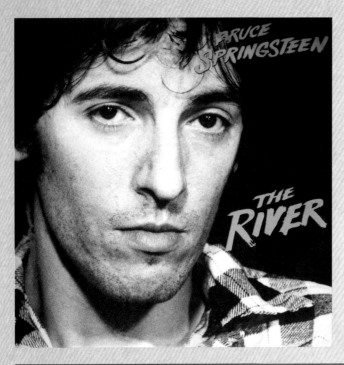

PRODUCER: Jon Landau, Bruce Springsteen, Steven Van Zandt

RECORDED: Power Station Studios, New York City

UK: 2

USA: 1

SIDE ONE
1. The Ties That Bind
2. Sherry Darling
3. Jackson Cage
4. Two Hearts
5. Independence Day

SIDE TWO
1. Hungry Heart
2. Out in the Street
3. Crush on You
4. You Can Look (But You Better Not Touch)
5. I Wanna Marry You
6. The River

SIDE THREE
1. Point Blank
2. Cadillac Ranch
3. I'm A Rocker
4. Fade Away
5. Stolen Car

SIDE FOUR
1. Ramrod
2. The Price You Pay
3. Drive All Night
4. Wreck on the Highway

A blowout double-album, split evenly between huge party numbers (and a wealth of live staples) and darker, real-world tales in the vein of the title track, 'The River' represented a Springsteen out to explore the emerging dualities of his music. And it floods rather than simply flows with themes of despair, inspiration, heartbreak, and joy as he sheds his old skin and slides comfortably into a new one. A collation of the many songs that never found their way onto his previous four albums, the tracks shift from cheerful, even celebratory, numbers to more intimate and/or melancholic compositions. 'The Ties That Bind', with its haunting chorus, launches the first disc in a light-hearted folky mood. The positivity continues in tracks such as 'Sherry Darling' with its molten saxophone, the energetic 'Out In The Street' with Steve Van Zandt's trademark vocal harmonies, and the simple and catchy 'Crush On You'. Then there's the scathing 'Jackson Cage', reflecting the irreversible mark that society can put on us according to our past actions. Hungry Heart' – originally meant for The Ramones – is another more upbeat track and Springsteen's first hit single. In the midst of the mostly dynamic tracks, some more delicate songs deal with real life stories such as 'Independence Day' in which Springsteen sings about his relationship with his father. The second album gives more space

to melancholic tracks, although a few more cheerful moments manage to bring a bit of freshness, such as the unforgettable and haunting 'Cadillac Ranch', or the catchy 'I'm A Rocker' and 'Ramrod'. The mid-tempo 'Point Blank' and 'Fade Away' tell of love stories gone wrong while the sleeker 'Stolen Car' observes the failure of a marriage and the eight minutes' long 'Drive All Night' is about a lost but enduring love. More classic in subject matter, 'The Price You Pay' and 'Wreck on The Highway' keep the emotional level at its highest. To surmise, despite its imposing format, 'The River' captivates with its different themes, tempo and atmospheres keeping the listener enraptured throughout. Laughing, crying and yelling with frustration all at once, it's about all you can ask for from a rock n roll album – plus a bit more. Call it a new beginning, an evolution or a shift of sorts, but Springsteen's artistic vision was never clearer than on 'The River'.

The Ties That Bind: The River Collection (2015)

'The Ties That Bind: The River Collection' was released in December 2015. A comprehensive look at 'The River' era, the set contains 52 tracks on four CDs with a wealth of unreleased material, and four hours of never-before-seen video on three DVDs.

Nebraska **1982**

PRODUCER: Bruce Springsteen

RECORDED: Colt's Neck, New Jersey

UK: 3

USA: 3

SIDE ONE
1. Nebraska
2. Atlantic City
3. Mansion on the Hill
4. Johnny 99
5. State Trooper

SIDE TWO
1. Used Cars
2. Open All Night
3. My Father's House
4. Reason to Believe

Recorded on cassette with just an acoustic guitar, a harmonica, a glockenspiel, and a synth over just a few days, these folk-influenced tracks didn't translate with a full band or in the studio, so the raw demos were released as a full album. The result? A tour de force of song-writing and storytelling that's unrivalled in rock. The song structures, melodies, and arrangements are simple - often just three chords, vocals, and a harmonic. Simplicity is key to the album's atmosphere, with writing that's compelling enough to attract attention without feeling overwrought. 'Atlantic City', 'Johnny 99', and 'Up All Night' are bangers with a sing-along choruses, but they never break the sense of tension that gives the album its soul. Each track is a miniature world, full of scenes, places, landscapes, fear, murder, and disappointment. The title track vividly recounts the story of Charles Starkweather and his killing spree through Wyoming. 'My Father's House' describes a nightmare full of demons and an absentee father. 'Highway Patrolman' is about strained family ties and duty condensed into a haunting five-minute ballad. You come away feeling like you know these characters - or that you might just be one yourself. 'Nebraska' isn't perfect. 'Mansion on the Hill' and 'Used Cars', while beautiful songs, aren't as compelling as the already mentioned highlights. And 'Open All Night', is maybe just a tad light-hearted to be included here. Overall, however, these 'lows' are far outweighed by the depth and heart of the rest of the songs. Nebraska is a rewarding musical experience that grows more and more profound with each listen. It is a glimpse into the meanness of the world and the humanity of its characters.

Born In The USA 1984

PRODUCER: Jon Landau, Bruce Springsteen, Chuck Plotkin, Steven Van Zandt

RECORDED: Power Station Studios, New York City; Hit Factory, New York City

UK: 1

USA: 1

SIDE ONE	SIDE TWO
1. Born in the USA	1. No Surrender
2. Cover Me	2. Bobby Jean
3. Darlington County	3. I'm Goin' Down
4. Working on the Highway	4. Glory Days
5. Downbound Train	5. Dancing in the Dark
6. I'm on Fire	6. My Hometown

Bruce Springsteen had become increasingly downcast as a songwriter during his recording career, and his pessimism bottomed out with previous album, 'Nebraska'. Although musically far more upbeat, 'Born in the U.S.A.', his massive triumph which threw off seven Top Ten hits and became one of the best-selling albums of all time, trafficked in much the same struggle. That the Reagan regime attempted to co-opt the title track as an election-year campaign song wasn't surprising but the song, like the album, is anything but a celebration of the Stars and Stripes and the pride and joy in being an American. The struggle to make that clear has actually been a central part of the album's legacy. Beneath the fanfare, 'Born in the U.S.A.' is an indictment of the Vietnam War and the neglect of veterans. But Springsteen also softened his message with nostalgia and sentimentality. More than anything else, 'Born in the U.S.A.' marked the first time that Springsteen's characters really seemed to relish the fight and to have something to fight for. In 'No Surrender' they

refuse to be defeated, in 'Bobby Jean' they have friendship and in 'My Hometown' they have family to defend.. The restless hero of "Dancing in the Dark" even pledges himself in the face of futility, and for Springsteen, that was a step forward. The 'romantic young boys' of his first two albums, chastened by 'the working life' endured on his third, fourth and fifth albums, and having faced the despair of his sixth, were still alive on this, his seventh, with their sense of humour and their determination intact. Critical and commercial success came together with 'Born in the USA' transforming the Boss into a global superstar, up there with the greats. The title track is self-described as one of his best songs. Regarded as the turning-point album in Bruce's career, by 2012, it had sold 30 million copies, making it one of the highest-selling albums of all time.

Tunnel of Love 1987

PRODUCER: Bruce Springsteen

RECORDED: A & M, Los Angeles; Kren Studios, Hollywood; Hit Factory, New York City; New Jersey.

UK: 1

USA: 1

SIDE ONE
1. Aint Got You
2. Tougher Than The Rest
3. All That Heaven Will Allow
4. Spare Parts
5. Cautious Man
6. Walk Like A Man

SIDE TWO
1. Tunnel of Love
2. Two Faces
3. Brilliant Disguise
4. One Step Up
5. When You're Alone
6. Valentine's Day

By 1987, Bruce had it all - money, fame, and a seemingly happy marriage to Hollywood actress Julianne Phillips. But inside, things were beginning to fray. His deep-seated insecurities were beginning to manifest as he began to have doubts about the future of his marriage and the direction of his career. Within two years of this release, he had divorced Julianne and dispensed with the E Street Band, opening up a new period for him. What makes 'Tunnel Of Love' such a challenging yet rewarding listen is the honesty and intimacy with which Bruce tackles such issues. Songs like the title track, 'Brilliant Disguise' and 'One Step Up' show a man who is fragile, vulnerable, and lacking in confidence - a stark contrast to the hyper-masculine Rambo type of the 'Born In The U.S.A.' era. The album's title track takes a familiar image of love, the carnival ride that gives it its name, and twists it so that it's other interpretation - a dark, unpredictable vortex with twists and turns along the way – cleverly becomes the focal point of the song. While a dark cloud looms over much of the album, particularly the latter half, Bruce also explores the more joyful, innocent areas of romance. 'Tougher

Than the Rest' - boasting a shimmering arrangement and one of Bruce's most intimate vocals - is a fantastic love song about commitment, strength and accepting your lover at face value. 'Walk Like A Man' is one of the most personal songs he had ever written thus far, recalling his wedding day and how his father must have felt watching his son take the same trip he had taken some 40 years earlier. In 'Cautious Man' he describes how letting go of these fears can only be done by confronting them head-on, and 'When You're Alone' is so simple yet so profound in its portrayal of a love that's dying. In a way, 'Tunnel of Love' marked a return to the simple folk/Americana form, albeit with a big, 80s-style production. Although touring with the E Street Band to promote the album in 1988, the band were not credited as a collective on this release and Springsteen was not to make another studio album with his backing band until 2002's 'The Rising'.

Human Touch
1992

PRODUCER: Jon Landau, Bruce Springsteen,
Chuck Plotkin, Roy Bittan

RECORDED: A & M, Los Angeles

UK: 1

USA: 2

TRACK LIST

1. Human Touch
2. Soul Driver
3. 57 Channels (And Nothin' On)
4. Cross My Heart
5. Gloria's Eyes
6. With Every Wish
7. Roll of the Dice
8. Real World
9. All or Nothin' at All
10. Man's Job
11. I Wish I Were Blind
12. The Long Goodbye
13. Real Man
14. Pony Boy

By the 1990s, Bruce Springsteen was one of the biggest names in music and one of the biggest stars in rock, with brilliant albums such as 'Born to Run' and 'Born in the U.S.A' and many other great, if not so popular ones, such as 'Nebraska' and 'The Wild, the Innocent & the E Street Shuffle'. But the Bruce of 1992 was a different beast to the one encountered in his earlier work. This is where 'Human Touch' comes in. Originally intended for release in 1990, Springsteen shelved the project until he had completed twin album, 'Lucky Town'. Of the two works released on the same March day in 1992, 'Human Touch' was the better selling, beating 'Lucky Town' to the number two slot on the US Billboard Charts. The majority of the tracks on 'Tunnel of Love' had dealt with the break-down of Bruce's first marriage but by '92, he had divorced and gone on to marry E Street Band member, Patti Scialfa. He was happy but happiness, for Springsteen, didn't necessarily inspire him to pen great songs. On 'Human Touch', with nothing driving Springsteen, he managed to achieve a grand total of. . .well, not a lot.

Bruce's early work was often based on political and economic incidents, the exception being 'Tunnel of Love'. These topics are non-existent on 'Human Touch', having been being replaced with much more lovey-dovey topics, such as love and, er, love. In fairness, the lead self-titled single is catchy and keeps it simple with low key guitars and quiet drumming. Bruce's USP had always been the ability to capture the imagination of his audience and to put into words and music their life experiences but songs like 'Cross my Heart' and 'All or Nothin' at all' are – for him - bland and uninspired. Without the E Street Band to give the music some depth and power, the backing is, for the most part, drab. A few songs manage to break the mould, though. 'Gloria's Eyes' actually has decent guitar parts to it, but the drum machine that makes up the backing track is boring and repetitive while the bass is almost non-existent. These criticisms are true for much of this album. However, Springsteen's voice is as good as it has ever been and if the music had been better, then perhaps the album would have been too. Then again, maybe not. . .

Lucky Town
1992

PRODUCER: Jon Landau, Bruce Springsteen,
Chuck Plotkin, Roy Bittan

RECORDED: Thrill Hill Studios, Colts Hill, New
Jersey; A & M, Los Angeles

UK: 2

USA: 3

TRACK LIST

1. Better Days
2. Lucky Town
3. Local Hero
4. If I Should Fall Behind
5. Leap of Faith
6. The Big Muddy
7. Living Proof
8. Book of Dreams
9. Souls of the Departed
10. My Beautiful Reward

Bruce Springsteen performing, 1992

The companion album to "Human Touch" , 'Lucky Town', it must be said, is a marked improvement to its twin. Written in just three weeks and recorded by Bruce alone (he plays all instruments except piano and drums where noted) in just as many, it was an afterthought of sorts that came to be only after 'Human Touch' was already in the can. While 'Lucky Town' feels a bit rushed, a little uneven, and underproduced and developed in places, it has, for all its shortcomings, several strengths, helping it rise above being a small personal album so that it is actually a good piece of work. Mature, forgiving, confessional, and the sign of a rebirth for this artist, 'Lucky Town' offers a unique glimpse into this man who was once born to run but who was now settling down and learning to live with himself, his new life with wife and family, and his troubled past. And it's about as up close and personal as he has ever been on record. 'Better Days', chronicling Bruce's recent loves, losses and eventual redemption, is a loud and celebratory track, followed by playful and knowing hometown song 'Local Hero'. In the tender, heart-felt ballad 'If I Should Fall Behind', he promises commitment and devotion to his new love, Patti, and these confessions of romantic desire continue on the next track in the spirited and soulful "Leap Of Faith". The second half of the record begins on a darker note with the cautionary tale 'The Big Muddy', which finds Bruce breaking out slide guitar and a very foreboding bass sound. We then move on to a song of inspirational and emotional faith restored in the form of 'Living Proof' with the wordsmith recounting his journey through heartbreak, loss, loneliness and fear before coming out on top. It is as good a straight forward rock song as Springsteen ever recorded. Finishing up the album, we are treated to yet another song of romantic commitment to his new wife in the thoughtful and quiet ballad 'Book Of Dreams' while with the stunning 'My Beautiful Reward', Springsteen reveals more of himself than ever before as he recounts his past sins, his search of relief and redemption, his own losses, struggles, and pain in life.

'The Ghost of Tom Joad'
1995

PRODUCER: Bruce Springsteen, Chuck Plotkin
RECORDED: Thrill Hill, New Jersey
UK: 16
USA: 11

TRACK LIST

1. The Ghost of Tom Joad
2. Straight Time
3. Highway 29
4. Youngstown
5. Sinaloa Cowboys
6. The Line
7. Balboa Park
8. Dry Lightning
9. The New Timer
10. Across the Border
11. Galveston Bay
12. My Best Was Never Good Enough

The 90s are often regarded by fans as a difficult patch for the Boss. Having attained such stature to almost become mythical in the previous decades, Springsteen had become not only a national treasure but also a walking embodiment of the American dream. 'The Ghost of Tom Joad', an album of broadly acoustic story-telling musings and blue-collar fantasies was never going to be numbered alongside the mighty 'Born To Run' nor does it carry the emotional depth of 'Darkness On The Edge of Town'. Of all the albums produced without the E Street Band however, 'The Ghost of Tom Joad' is perhaps the most intelligent, poignant and sincere of any of Springsteen's less acclaimed work. Framed/ inspired by its title character, it serves as a parched, narrative-driven consideration of poverty, immigration and the brittle troubles of Americans and Mexicans in the Southwest. Sparse acoustic backdrops, layered with subtle organs, strings and harmonicas make up most of the album's music, allowing Springsteen's distinctive voice and storytelling to guide the ebb and flow of the music. This is the Boss at his most soulful and sincere, quietly strumming out tales of desperate Mexican migrants or blue-collar workers left behind in backwater towns. 'The Ghost of Tom Joad' should not be overlooked. If nothing else, the album provides a truly immersive texture and finds Springsteen's sensibilities at their most earnest.

The Rising
2002

PRODUCER: Brendan O'Brien
RECORDED: Southern Tracks Studio, Atlanta, Georgia
UK: 1
USA: 1

TRACK LIST

1. Lonesome Day
2. Into the Fire
3. Waitin' on a Sunny Day
4. Nothing Man
5. Countin' on a Miracle
6. Empty Sky
7. Worlds Apart
8. Let's Be Friends (Skin to Skin)
9. Further On (Up the Road)
10. The Fuse
11. Mary's Place
12. You're Missing
13. The Rising
14. Paradise
15. My City of Ruins

At some point during the weeks following the 9/11 attacks, the Boss was reportedly strolling out on the beach in his native Asbury Park when a stranger approached him and said, "We need you now." Springsteen clearly took the advice to heart as the next summer he released 'The Rising'. This – his 12th studio album – didn't just succeed at helping to numb America's pain, it essentially revitalized Springsteen's career. How? By recalling the E Street Band and returning to his key themes of faith, hope, loss and the creation of strength gleaned from each other. From the first strings of 'Lonesome Day', it's clear that 'The Rising' is a bittersweet affair. Simultaneously optimistic but burdened by the weight of reality, the stunning opener showcases confident, upbeat song-writing with a lingering subtext of sadness. This is achieved just as effectively in 'Waitin' on a Sunny Day', 'Countin' on a Miracle', and the record's infectious hit title track. On these cuts, Springsteen's role is one of comfort and support, often attempting to console in situations that are practically inconsolable. Shifting perspectives song by song - some likely autobiographical, some not so - at no point does Bruce look outward for blame, preferring the high road to the easy path. There's no blindly patriotic call against foreign perpetrators or those who look like them. Instead, as he's done his whole career, Springsteen focuses on ordinary people - in this case, the families of those who awoke to missing loved ones and the community leaders trying to engage with those in need. If there's one point that looks beyond the American homeland, it's the stellar mid-album duo of 'Empty Sky' and 'Worlds Apart' - the former a bitter, confused rumination on whether revenge causes closure or only more emptiness; the latter a Middle Eastern-tinged helping of Americana that aspires to not let cultural differences destroy our basic humanity. Complete with backing Qawwali singers and an incredibly emotional guitar solo by Steven Van Zandt, 'Worlds Apart' is also arguably 'The Rising' at its most innovative. 'Nothing Man' adopts the perspective of a depressed hero with survivor's guilt, while 'You're Missing' details the emptiness felt at home when you know a loved one will never come back. The desolate, soul-crushing 'Paradise' takes this sensation one step further. Being placed back-to-back with the more exuberant, reassuring tracks like 'Countin' on a Miracle' and 'The Rising' only serve to spotlight how easy it can be to slip back into the darkness when you're alone.

Devils & Dust
2005

PRODUCER: Brendan O'Brien, Bruce Springsteen, Chuck Plotkin
RECORDED: Thrill Hill Studios, Colts Neck, New Jersey
UK: 1
USA: 1

TRACK LIST

1. Devils and Dust
2. All the Way Home
3. Reno
4. Long Time Comin'
5. Black Cowboys
6. Maria's Bed
7. Silver Palomino
8. Jesus Was an Only Son
9. Leah
10. The Hitter
11. All I'm Thinkin' About
12. Matamoros Banks

This acoustic, primarily solo outing, mixing themes both familial and political, followed the extensive tour for 'The Rising'. Many of the songs on 'Devils. . .' were part of the Springsteen archive – eg, "All the Way Home" was written for Southside Johnny in 1991 while 'Long Time Coming' and 'The Hitter' date back to the time of Tom Joad. Other songs were a new departure for Springsteen – the lyrically controversial 'Reno' caused a few raised eyebrows with its mention of anal sex, for instance. While the characters that roam through 'Devils & Dust' are similarly heartbroken, desperate, and downtrodden to those described on 'Nebraska' and 'The Ghost of Tom Joad', they also differ. Several hail from the West, some are despairing, some dare to be hopeful, there is even a happy couple. Springsteen's writing is similarly varied, occasionally hearkening back to the bleak-like lyrics of 'Nebraska' but it's mostly densely composed, assured, and evocative – almost as if the songs were meant to be read aloud rather than sung. But the key to' Devils & Dust' is that the sonics are as vivid and varied as the words. Downbeat epics like 'The Hitter' or the sad, lonely 'Reno' are juxtaposed against the lighter 'Long Time Comin', 'Maria's Bed' and 'All I'm Thinkin' About' while the moodier 'Black Cowboys' and the title track are enhanced by a subtle yet big production. It results in an album record that's far removed in feel from 'Nebraska'. 'Devils and Dust' is also concise and precisely constructed, two things the otherwise excellent 2002 comeback 'The Rising' fell down on in parts. This sharp focus helped make this album, many critics felt, the leanest, most artistic Springsteen work in many years.

We Shall Overcome: The Seeger Sessions
2006

PRODUCER: Bruce Springsteen
RECORDED: Thrill Hill Studios, Colts Neck, New Jersey
UK: 3
USA: 3

TRACK LIST

1. Old Dan Tucker	8. My Oklahoma Home
2. Jesse James	9. Eyes on the Prize
3. Mrs McGrath	10. Shenandoah
4. O Mary Don't You Weep	11. Pay Me My Money Down
5. John Henry	12. We Shall Overcome
6. Erie Canal	13. Froggie Went A-Courtin'
7. Jacob's Ladder	

Ditching The E Street band once again and taking up with the 17 member Seeger Sessions Band, this collection of traditional folk music is given the big band treatment by Springsteen. The instruments range from guitar to banjo to washboard to accordion, tuba, trumpet and piano. Violin and pedal steel guitar are also on hand. And if you listen carefully, there's even the sound of someone blowing over the top of an empty whiskey jug. The Seeger Sessions band do a sterling job of laying down a country/rock vibe where necessary but they also know when to back off. Professionally recorded in Springsteen's New Jersey home (in his living room, to be precise) over the course of just three days, the album – although containing numbers with a serious slant such as 'Shenandoah', Civil Rights anthem 'We Shall Overcome' and old negro spiritual gospel 'Mary, Don't You Weep No More' - has a spontaneous, upbeat, celebratory, down-home, foot-stopping, hand-clapping feel to it. This is not quiet folk music. Nor is it stuck in a folkie rut. Healthy doses of gospel, blues, Dixieland, and other influences also abound. And it's all delivered via a large band and a robust bandleader with a big voice who is more than up to the task of interpreting these traditional songs anew to a new generation of listeners. This time around, 'spinned' by Bruce Springsteen and a top-notch band with just enough regard for tradition, but adding a bit more life to the mix, these old songs collated by Pete Seeger are reborn and serve as a reminder that in the course of history, sometimes, what goes around, comes around.

Bruce Springsteen at the Northrup Auditorium, 1996

Magic
2007

PRODUCER: Brendan O'Brien
RECORDED: Southern Track Studios, Atlanta, Georgia
UK: 1
USA: 1

TRACK LIST

1. Radio Nowhere
2. You'll Be Comin' Down
3. Livin' in the Future
4. Your Own Worst Enemy
5. Gypsy Biker
6. Girls in their Summer Clothes
7. I'll Work for Your Love
8. Magic
9. Last to Die
10. Long Walk Home
11. Devil's Arcade

Springsteen reconvened the E Street Band for 11 new songs on 'Magic', noting that the album's title refers to the '*times when what's true can be made to seem like a lie, and what's a lie can be made to seem true*'. Once again produced by alternative / modern rock producer Brendan 'O Brien whom Bruce had employed for The Rising in 2002, 'Magic' is not much short of what its title might suggest. After the opening rock number, the album quickly shifts to something perhaps unexpected at this point in Springsteen's career. It harkens back to early Springsteen – the Bruce of romantic visions, whimsical melodies, grand pop songs, and fiery R&B, the kind of which you can find on his first three albums. 'Magic' is in the line-up of any classic Springsteen album you may care to mention. That's not to say that this is a work of nostalgia, rather, an album of modern sounds and pleasant surprises - the first of which comes early on as the band moves from the raucous, hard-driving rock sound that is 'Radio Nowhere' and recalls Bruce's late 70's - early '80's work to the smooth Byrds influenced pop of 'You'll Be Coming Down'. This track is full of lush vocal harmonies set against long time Springsteen sax man Clarence Clemons' outstanding horn playing. 'Magic' is a very 'catchy' album. Clemons' soulful sax on 'Living In The Future', coupled with Bruce's funky guitar work and keyboardist Danny Federici's glockenspiel, recalls the 'Born to Run' rhythm and blues of 'Tenth Avenue Freeze Out'. Meanwhile 'I'll Work for You' features a whimsical lead in piano reminiscent of many Bruce songs past. But as already stated, this is not a work of nostalgia but a superb and *mature* work by one of rock's all-time greats, a man devoid of pretence, self-consciousness, or the shallow rock trappings of the day. 'Magic' flows and is an easy, entertaining listen from start to finish. When questioned about the theme of this album, Springsteen replied, '*It's The Byrds, The Beach Boys, a California album*'. That it is. But it is also an album that lyrically threads human loss and dislocation throughout, and the politics that sometimes accompanies these things. It is this common thread that not only pulls the record tightly together tight, but lends it weight, as well.

Working on a Dream
2009

PRODUCER: Brendan O'Brien
RECORDED: Southern Track Studios, Atlanta, Georgia
UK: 1
USA: 1

TRACK LIST

1. Outlaw Pete
2. My Lucky Day
3. Working on a Dream
4. Queen of the Supermarket
5. What Love Can Do
6. This Life
7. Good Eye
8. Tomorrow Never Knows
9. Life Itself
10. Kingdom of Days
11. Surprise, Surprise
12. The Last Carnival
13. The Wrestler

After 'Magic', Springsteen – as was his way - just couldn't stop writing songs and 'Working on a Dream' is the result of that output. It explores a classic pop sound for a release date coinciding with the historic inauguration of President Barack Obama. The fourth studio album Springsteen made in collaboration with the producer Brendan O'Brien, it continues the practice of producing songs in which the musical trademarks of the E Street Band are outnumbered by adventures into areas not previously associated with Springsteen. The string orchestra that made its appearance on a couple of tracks of 2007's 'Magic', for instance, returns in various forms on this album, joined by a variety of sounds and approaches seemingly gleaned from the young Springsteen's record collection - the Beach Boys harmonies on 'This Life', for example, the jangling Byrds-like guitars on 'Life Itself' and the 'I Am the Walrus-style' fadeout of 'Queen of the Supermarket'.

At its heart, 'Working on a Dream' is an ambitious album – some would say overproduced with over-the-top orchestration, particularly on 'My Lucky Day' and 'What Love Can Do'. There are several musical genres at play here. Eight-minute epic 'Outlaw Pete' sounds like an Americana/Tex Mex kind of number with a harmonica in the style of Ennio Morricone; the bluesy 'Good Eye' sounds like it came straight out of Mississippi while 'Tomorrow Never Knows' is good old country/pop a la Nashville; and 'Surprise, Surprise' blasts a Phil Spector-like wall of sound. The poignant 'The Last Carnival' is easily the best track of the album – it's a soft acoustic track that doubles as a heartfelt tribute to former E Street Band organ player Danny Federici, who passed away in 2008 from skin cancer. Springsteen sings in his lowest registers for 'The Last Carnival' and sounds like he's choking up as he's singing. No doubt he was.

Wrecking Ball
2012

PRODUCER: Ron Aniello, Bruce Springsteen
RECORDED: Stone Hill, Colts Neck, New Jersey
UK: 1
USA: 1

TRACK LIST

1. We Take Care of Our Own
2. Easy Money
3. Shackled and Drawn
4. Jack of All Trades
5. Death to My Hometown
6. This Depression
7. Wrecking Ball
8. You've Got It
9. Rocky Ground
10. Land of Hope and Dreams
11. We Are Alive

In the wake of the world financial meltdown of 2008. Springsteen returned to social commentary for his 17th studio album – the theme being songs about characters living at the edge of the American abyss in the face of growing disparity between rich and poor. The 11 tracks feature uber-gritty vocals and gut-punching lyrics paired with a sonic palette that is a tapestry of folk, gospel, rock, Celtic, country and hip hop. Yes, hip hop. In 'Rocky Ground' - with its hip hop Fugees-like sound, Gospel-like samples, choirs and guest vocalist Michelle Moore – Springsteen is exploring new territory. However, harking back, opening track, 'We Take Care of Our Own', borrows from the 'Born in the USA' playbook and is heard as a political anthem. This sets the stage for an album in which

Springsteen puts the capitalist leaders and fat-cat bankers of his country on trial. We journey with him on a tour of an economically depressed American landscape that sways back and forth between fanfare and lamentation. 'Jack of all Trades' is a slow ballad tinged with horns, and a solo from guest guitarist Tom Morello on 'Death to my Hometown' is an Irish folk foot-stomper. The title track then steers the album into a search for redemption with the acknowledgment that, as they always have and always will, *hard times come and hard times go'*. However, this album is not without a few question marks. 'You've Got It' has the feel of a song that missed the cut on 'Born in the USA' and, coincidentally, marks the only departure from 'Wrecking Balls' core themes. The

SiriusXM's celebration of 10 years of satellite radio with a concert by Bruce Springsteen and The E Street Band at The Apollo Theater, New York, March 9, 2012

rap sequence on 'Rocky Road' also comes across as being included solely for the sake of having rap on the album. 'Wrecking Ball' roars back with 'Land of Hopes and Dreams', featuring familiar soaring saxophone from the late Clarence Clemons, who passed away from post-stroke complications in June 2011. In the final track, the Johnny Cash inspired 'We are Alive', the message is that while death is inevitable, it's not the end. There could be no more fitting eulogy to Clemons.

High Hopes
2014

PRODUCER: Ron Aniello, Brendan O'Brien, Bruce Springsteen

RECORDED: 301 Studios, Byron Bay, Australia; Southern Track Studios, Atlanta, Georgia; Stone Hill, Colts Neck, New Jersey.

UK: 1

USA: 1

TRACK LIST

1. High Hopes	7. Frankie Fell in Love
2. Harry's Place	8. This is your Sword
3. American Skin (41 shots)	9. Hunter of Invisible Game
4. Just Like Fire Would	10. The Ghost of Tom Joad
5. Down in the Hole	11. The Wall
6. Heaven's Wall	12. Dream Baby Dream

Springsteen's 18th studio album was a different sort of release for him. It featured both original and cover songs that had been performed live over the years, some never recorded in a studio setting, as well as a few older songs reconceived with new arrangements and new musicians – including 'Rage Against the Machine guitarist Tom Morello, who had joined the Boss and the E Street Band on their 2013 tour of Australia and also made contributions to 'Wrecking Ball'. However, the result is something of a mixed bag, a little disjointed and, at times, aimless – especially the middle section which is filled with forgettable songs that sound like leftovers from Springsteen's string of noughties records. Not that there aren't strong songs scattered among the occasionally flimsy frames, including stage favourite 'American Skin (41 Shots),' originally written in 1999 and one of Springsteen's best songs of the past 15 years, which, for this album, was finally put down in the studio. The pair of covers which open and close the album are also strong - the Havalinas' title track, which Springsteen first recorded on a 1995 EP, and Suicide's 'Dream Baby Dream,' respectively. There are other enjoyable and catchy songs, such as' Just Like Fire Would' and 'Frankie Fell in Love', but amongst these 'This Is Your Sword' is the most impressive, with its folky rythms, bagpipes and banjo, faithfully played according to its Celtic origins. Best of all the tracks, though, is a re-worked, full band version of 'The Ghost of Tom Joad' which features Morello unleash some raw electric fury. Poignantly, the skills of the late Clarence Clemons and the late Danny Federici also feature on several tracks.

Western Stars
2019

PRODUCER: Ron Aniello, Bruce Springsteen

RECORDED: Stone Hill, Colts Neck, New Jersey

UK: 1

USA: 2

TRACK LIST

1. Hitch Hikin'	8. Sundown
2. The Wayfarer	9. Somewhere North of Nashville
3. Tucson Train	10. Stones
4. Western Stars	11. There Goes My Miracle
5. Sleepy Joe's Café	12. Hello Sunshine
6. Drive Fast (The Stuntman)	13. Moonlight Motel
7. Chasin' Wild Horses	

Bruce Springsteen's 19th studio album 'Western Stars' marked his first new studio record in five years and drew its inspiration from the Southern California pop records of the late '60s and early '70s. Think Burt Bacharach and Glen Campbell. Given its laid-back vibe, Charles Giordano was the only E Street Band instrumentalist to play on this album, although Scialfa and Tyrell provided backing vocals. In a hark back to the 1970s, alumni David Sancious also made a contribution. The album's very best songs have Bruce successfully returning the piercing, vivid character studies whose surroundings, situations, and scars - both physically and spiritually – he makes come to life in a technicolour, cinematic fashion.

These include the 'past his prime' actor of the title song and the wounded but persistent troubadour of "The Stuntman" - classic flawed Springsteen protagonists, both. Then there's 'Moonlight Motel' – a truly haunting ballad in which the Boss so sensitively portrays loneliness and regret. Not quite so memorable are the likes of obvious filler 'Hitch 'Hikin', cringey ballad 'Stones', the diluted 'Smoky Joe's Café' and the one-dirge-too-many 'Chasin' Wild Horses'. Musicality-wise, the album boasts a sweeping, grand sound, with lots of lush strings and triumphant horns coming in midway through each song. 'Western Stars' may not be a star album but it is a return to form for The Boss.

Letter To You
2020

PRODUCER: Ron Aniello, Bruce Springsteen
RECORDED: Thrill Hill, Colts Neck, New Jersey, US
UK: 1
USA: 2

TRACK LIST

1. One Minute You're Here
2. Letter to You
3. Burnin' Train
4. Janey Needs a Shooter
5. Last Man Standing
6. The Power of Prayer
7. House of a Thousand Guitars
8. Rainmaker
9. If I Was the Priest
10. Ghosts
11. Song for Orphans
12. I'll See You in My Dreams

'Letter to You', both the title track and album, is Springsteen's meditation on a life lived and his own mortality. The album is also about coming home, both literally and metaphorically. Recording in November 2019 in Springsteen's home studio in New Jersey, the E-Street Band – reunited with their leader for the first time since 2016 – impress with a performance reminiscent of past glories. They play 'live' in that each track is recorded as a band with minimal overdubs. This creates a real pulsating energy, driven by Max Weinberg's dramatic propulsive drumming and the guitars of Steve Van Zandt, Nils Lofgren and Springsteen himself. And it took just five days to get in the can with Springsteen hailing it as *'one of the greatest recording experiences I've ever had'*. The group complement each other in endless ways and are particularly on form during 'Last Man Standing' and 'Burnin' Train', filling in the non-vocal passages with their signature, show-stopping instrumentation. Some of the tracks have especially memorable lyrical sequences. One such number is the sombre opener 'One Minute You're Here' in which Springsteen softly sings *'I took all my fears and doubts / In my letter to you / All the hard things that I found out / In my letter to you'*. Another favourite is 'Ghosts', in which Springsteen speaks about a fellow musician whose presence can be felt everywhere despite having passed away. The most likely individual is George Theiss – who played with him in 'The Castiles' and who had passed away in 2018. 'Letter to You' notably features three recordings of compositions from the 1970s that didn't see the light of day at the time – 'Janey Needs a Shooter', 'If I Was the Priest' and 'Song for Orphans'. We may be 50 years on, but the tracks pulsate with the energy they would have had when first written.

Only The Strong Survive
2022

PRODUCER: Ron Aniello, Bruce Springsteen
RECORDED: Thrill Hill, New Jersey
UK: To be confirmed
USA: To be confirmed

TRACK LIST

1. Only the Strong Survive
2. Soul Days (feat. Sam Moore)
3. Nightshift
4. Do I Love You (Indeed I Do)
5. The Sun Ain't Gonna Shine Anymore
6. Turn Back the Hands of Time
7. When She Was My Girl
8. Hey, Western Union Man
9. I Wish It Would Rain
10. Don't Play That Song
11. Any Other Way
12. I Forgot to Be Your Lover (featuring Sam Moore)
13. 7 Rooms of Gloom
14. What Becomes of the Brokenhearted
15. Someday We'll Be Together

Springsteen's 21st studio album with Columbia Records, 'Only the Strong Survive' is a solo release and collection of fifteen soul music greats celebrating soul music gems from the legendary catalogues of Motown, Gamble and Huff, Stax and many more.

'I wanted to make an album where I just sang,' says Springsteen. 'And what better music to work with than the great American songbook of the Sixties and Seventies? I've taken my inspiration from Levi Stubbs, David Ruffin, Jimmy Ruffin, the Iceman Jerry Butler, Diana Ross, Dobie Gray, and Scott Walker, among many others. I've tried to do justice to them all—and to the fabulous writers of this glorious music. My goal is for the modern audience to experience its beauty and joy, just as I have since I first heard it. I hope you love listening to it as much as I loved making it.'

This is a covers album, true, but it's a treat for the ears to hear.

Still from 2019's Western Stars documentary

RANKED

Springsteen Studio Albums Ranked

21 Human Touch

On March 31 1992, Bruce Springsteen released a pair of solo albums, the first in years with his E Street Band homies. Of the two, 'Human Touch' and 'Lucky Town', the former is the weaker and doesn't seem to flow organically. '57 Channels (And Nothin' On)' reveals itself as an uncharacteristically gauche attempt at social commentary.

20 High Hopes

Akin to a Springsteen outlet sale as rejected songs, cover versions and songs only previously performed live get the studio treatment. Features re-recordings of 'The Ghost of Tom Joad' and 'American Skin (41 Shots)' but the officially released live versions of both songs are thought by many to be superior, although Tom Morello's screaming guitar on the former track comes as a raunchy surprise. Also, an album half-comprised of covers was never going to come close to making the Springsteen top ten.

19 Only the Strong Survive

Springsteen's most recent release is an album made up entirely of classic soul covers like 'What Becomes of the Broken Hearted', 'The Night Shift' and 'Someday We'll Be Together'. It's a love letter to these greats, the musical arrangements are lush and swoonful, and his voice sounds sublime, especially when you consider this guy is in his 70s. But the bottom line is he didn't write the material.

18 Lucky Town

Considerably superior to his other 1992 solo releases, 'Lucky Town' is an up-close-and-personal Springsteen laid bare. Recorded in just three weeks, it feels a tad rushed, a little uneven, and underproduced and under developed in places while the quality of song-writing isn't that consistent. However, 'If I Should Fall Behind' is a truly beautiful ballad, more than fulfilling Springsteen's prophecy about it being 'One of my best songs about the dedication to one another that comes with love.'

17 Working on A Dream

Springsteen's first album of the Obama era, 'Working on A Dream' is in most respects a companion to the Magic recordings. Good vibes it may have but it's a tad Springsteen-light and somewhat devoid of the Boss' legendary energy.

16 Wrecking Ball

Bruce Springsteen's 17th studio album is something of a protest vote with songs tackling hypocrisy, greed, and corruption set to a musical backing of Civil War-type drums snares, gospel choruses, and chain-gang stomps. Hip hop track 'Rocky Ground', featuring Michelle Moore, while a surprising foray into hip-hop, sounds slightly gratuitous, while some feel included tracks 'Land Of Hope and Dreams' and 'American Land' were not in need of a re-record.

15 Devils and Dust

'Devils and Dust' reflects Springsteen's frustration with the 2003 Iraq War and the re-election of George W Bush. It's a folk-rock vibe that has the unenviable task of competing with the rest of Springsteen's vast acoustic songbook and its immediate predecessor, 'The Rising'.

14 Western Stars

His first album without The E Street Band since 'Devils and Dust' 14 years earlier, Springsteen described his 2019 cowboy album as an homage to old 'Southern California pop music' as pioneered by the likes of Burt Bacharach and Glen Campbell. Hailed as his best studio opus in years, 'Western Stars' is majestic in scale but traditional in subject matter and narrative.

13 A Letter to You

On his 20th studio album, Springsteen reflects on his past like never before and faces up to his own mortality. Following the autobiographical thread of his 2016 memoir and also his Broadway show, the album is almost like a Springsteen narrative, observing the ways that music sustains us through good times and bad. Recorded live, Bruce and the E Street Band give off an electric energy while 'Ghosts' is his next anthem in the making.

12 We Shall Overcome. The Seeger Sessions

A tribute album that sees Bruce let loose with a new team of musicians. The tracks sound boisterously fresh no matter the age of the material and by filling the album entirely with traditional folk songs, Bruce proves how relevant their themes remain while also establishing that his own originals belong here.

11 The Ghost of Tom Joad

Springsteen followed two slightly laboured and underwhelming solo albums in the form of 'Human Touch' and 'Lucky Town' with this understated opus highlighting the exploitation of American workers. He rediscovers his political commentator chops in 'Youngstown' – a track about an Ohio town on its uppers. The title track inspired an anarchic cover from 'Rage Against the Machine'.

10 Magic

The E Street Band are finally back with The Boss with the result that 'Magic', with its jacked-up bar band sound and meaningful lyricism, is arguably Springsteen's most feel-good album. Verging on the vanilla in parts, nevertheless Springsteen and the E boys' particular brand of dad-rock definitely delivers, inspiring up-and-coming indie bands like 'Arcade Fire' and 'The Killers'. 'Long Walk Home' offers a tad more depth.

9 Tunnel of Love

A quiet, often acoustic country-tinged album, 'Tunnel of Love' (released in 1987) was the first non-E Street Band album (excluding 'Nebraska') and marked a change in musical direction for Springsteen. Described as heartfelt and deep, it includes some of his most personal songs as he muses on love, marriage, misfortune and divorce. Nils Lofgren's cheesy guitar on the title track is very OTT '80s but 'Brilliant Disguise' and 'Tougher Than the Rest' are classics.

8 Greetings from Asbury Park, N.J.

Youthful enthusiasm, a certain naivety and raw talent makes Springsteen's debut album a gem. It's a sublime mix of acoustic folk, rock n' roll, jazz and R & B, and while his New Jersey tales can be haunted and tragic, as they are in 'Lost in the Flood', the songs are still imbued with romance and exuberance. Not the best song-writing Springsteen would ever do but none the worse for all that.

7 The Rising

Having spent most of the 1990s experimenting as a solo artist, Springsteen reunited with the E Street Band with an album which showcased his response to 9/11. 'My City of Ruins' and 'The Rising' are among the most poignant and emotional tracks in his entire songbook. Springsteen at the forefront of the zeitgeist and speaking directly to a nation in pain.

6 The Wild, the Innocent & the E Street Shuffle

Springsteen's grooviest record – a veritable funk/jazz fest with a side order of rock n roll, showcasing the E Street Band at their high-energy best. Check out the horn section on the title track, the waltzing accordion of '4th of July, Asbury Park (Sandy)', the luscious piano showcase on 'New York City Serenade'. . . This is Bruce as a musical tour-de-force and a reminder that he's at his best with his Jersey boys at his side.

5 The River

A double album spanning 20 tracks, 'The River' is not always consistent, with a few songs getting lost in the mix. Others, though, find Springsteen at his most eloquent, emotional and soulful – his feelings about moving away from his father on 'Independence Day', his brush with death on 'Wreck on The Highway', and the title track which speaks so eloquently of life's ups and downs. Lyrics apart, his mastery of musical genres on this album is truly awe-inspiring.

4 Born in The USA

At a first glance, Springsteen's mega-selling, mid '80s album is a celebration of all things American. False. The title is not a big up for being born in the States but rather a stiletto-like critique of a system that abuses its military before neglecting them as veterans. The infectious, stadia-friendly hooks of 'Dancing in the Dark' and 'Glory Days' are also juxtaposed with words of anxiety. Very, very smart.

3 Nebraska

In 1981, Springsteen left the E-Street band behind and recorded this album on cassette player. The complete antithesis of everything that had gone before, its 10 songs could easily be a part of the Bob Dylan canon - spare, acoustic, mythic, religious and dark. 'Nebraska' is a tribute to the downtrodden of America, proving Springsteen believes that for many, the American Dream never existed.

2 Darkness on The Edge of Town

Springsteen's first album post 'Appel-gate, both lyrically and musically, 'Darkness on The Edge Of Town' lives up to its brooding title. There is an edge and an anger to Springsteen and the E Street Band here that perhaps was never matched so consistently again. There is also a tight, concise feel to the tunes, with none of the musical wandering found on the first four albums. DOTEOT is not an easy listen. It's a record for hard times, finding room for resolve amid the shadows, yet contains some of the most meaningful songs in the Springsteen canon.

1 Born to Run

'Born To Run's' eight songs run to less than 40 minutes in length but as a whole, add up to one of the best albums ever made. Period. It's a classic, honest musical expression of hope, dreams and survival with a colossal wall of sound production that would have made Phil Spector proud. Clarence Clemons' triumphant yet plaintive sax playing and Roy Bittan's piano riffs complement the raunchy guitar sound with a side order of chiming glockenspiel - and the Boss's gritty vocals with their exquisitely evocative lyrics are the main course. Quite simply, a magnificent album that pays off on every bet ever placed on the boy from Freehold, New Jersey.

A Selection of the best Compilations, Live Albums, EPs, Box Sets and DVDs

Live 1975–85

Released November 1986

Clocking in at 40 songs and three CDs (and five vinyl records!), this insanely anticipated career-spanning set was a treasure chest for fans thirsting for a document of ten years of E Street shows. Bonus: It includes cuts such as 'Fire' and 'Because the Night' – live favourites that had yet to see the light of day on an official release.

Chimes of Freedom

Released August 1988

This four-track, live EP was released to benefit the Amnesty International 'Human Rights Now!' Tour. Springsteen announced his involvement in the tour during a show in Stockholm, just prior to the band's performance of Bob Dylan's 'Chimes of Freedom' as featured on the EP. Other tracks were selected from earlier tour stops in Detroit and Los Angeles.

Greatest Hits

Released February 1995

Bruce's first compilation album incorporates 14 of his best-known songs, along with his hit 'Streets of Philadelphia' from the film 'Philadelphia', which won multiple Grammys and an Academy Award. Also included is fan-favourite outtake 'Murder Incorporated' and three more songs newly recorded with a reunited E Street Band in January 1995.

Tracks

Released November 1998

A Bruce fan's nirvana - four discs of never-before-heard songs, demos, and B-sides, a treasure trove of material mostly left on the cutting-room floor from his early auditions for John Hammond through his work in the 1990s. Not a retrospective but an 'alternate road map' and a glimpse at the ambition, development, and prolific creativity of a rock icon.

18 Tracks

Released April 1999

An album that takes what is arguably the best from 'Tracks' and adds three more never-released titles, including the long-clamoured-for 'The Fever' and 'The Promise'. The latter was later released in its 1978 form on the 2010 box set of the same name, but here it's a stripped-down piano version Bruce recorded specifically for this sampler.

Live in New York City

(DVD) Released November 2001

This two-DVD set features the Emmy-award winning HBO broadcast from the final two shows of the E Street Band reunion tour from Madison Square Garden. A second disc compiles an additional 11 previously unseen songs from the shows. The set also features a documentary with live clips and interviews with the members of the E Street Band.

Live in Barcelona

Released November 2002

Recorded in 2002, partly broadcast on CBS and performed to a crowd best described as 'deliriously insane', 'Barcelona' captures the E Street Band with new addition Soozie Tyrell firing on all cylinders on the tour behind 'The Rising'. 'Live in Barcelona' marked the first time that a complete Springsteen show was released on either audio or video.

The Essential Bruce Springsteen
Released November 2003

Springsteen had an active hand in the selection of tracks for this three-disc greatest hits compilation, stating in the liner notes that *'We saw a lot of new faces on our recent tour, and we put this collection together with them in mind'*. The album spans his entire career and includes key hits and deep tracks, as well as an entire third disc devoted to rarities.

VH-1 Storytellers
Released September 2005

A DVD release of Springsteen's April 2005 performance, which featured the live debut of two songs from 'Devils & Dust'. Bruce performed on acoustic guitar and piano, with Patti Scialfa joining on backing vocals for 'Brilliant Disguise'. He discussed his writing process and the stories behind the songs, also taking questions from the audience.

Born to Run. 30th Anniversary Edition
Released November 2005

Those waiting for Springsteen reissue treatment to begin regarded this three-disc box with sheer glee - it featured a sterling remaster, a making-of doc, and his first full-length concert DVD, filmed in London at the height of '70s Bruce-mania that captured a band looking to live up to and demolish the hype.

Hammersmith Odeon, London '75
Released February 2006

The audio companion to the DVD release of the legendary November 18, 1975 concert at the Hammersmith Odeon in London, England — the European concert debut of Bruce Springsteen and the E Street Band. This is the only full-length, official release of the early band live on stage and contains essential performances of many E Street classics.

Live in Dublin
Released June 2007

Captures the final stand of the 18-piece Sessions Band as it roars through traditionals, re-sculpted folk numbers and radically reconfigured Springsteen originals — including a 10-minute big-band 'Open All Night' and a roof-raising 'Atlantic City' — all marinated in the sounds of New Orleans.

Live in Dublin Film
Released June 2007

If you think the Sessions Band sounded big, get a load of them in video form - 18 musicians onstage in front of a cosy but lively crowd that pretty much loses its mind at the mention of 'Irish' during 'American Land'.

Girls in their Summer Clothes EP
Released January 2008

'Girls in their Summer Clothes' from 2007's Magic, entered the Billboard Hot 100 and won the 2008 Grammy Award for Best Rock Song. This digital-only EP includes two audio tracks, the 'Winter Mix' and a live performance from the 2007 Magic tour, as well as the song's Mark Pellington-directed music video, filmed in Asbury Park and Ocean Grove, New Jersey.

Magic Tour Highlights
Released July 2008

Recorded during the 2008 Magic tour, with guests Alejandro Escovedo (Houston, April 14), Tom Morello (Anaheim, April 7) and Roger McGuinn (Orlando, April 23). 'Sandy' is taken from Danny Federici's last performance with the E Street Band (Indianapolis, March 20). Proceeds from sales of this digital-only EP benefitted the Danny Federici Melanoma Fund.

Greatest Hits
Released January 2009

The only compilation album crediting the E Street Band, 'Greatest Hits' was an exclusive Wal-Mart release. Dropping material recorded between 'Born in the U.S.A' and the E Street reunion, it adds songs from 'The Rising' and 'Magic', and, unlike 1995's 'Greatest Hits', offers a pre-'Born to Run' favourite, 'Rosalita'. A European version with an alternative track list was later released.

London Calling: Live in Hyde Park
Released June 2010

Recorded June 28, 2009 at London's Hyde Park, this concert film captures an E Street Band festival appearance from their 'Working on a Dream' world tour. Included are highlights of the 2009 set, including 'Seeds' and the sign-request portion of the show.

The Promise: The Darkness on the Edge of Town Story
Released November 2016

Three years elapsed between 'Born to Run' and 'Darkness' and this time was astonishingly prolific for Springsteen. This six-disc box set contains the remastered CD and 22 additional tracks, a '78 concert DVD, a feature-length documentary, and a newly filmed E Street Band performance of the album, illuminating one of The Boss' most richly rewarding periods.

The Promise
Released November 2016

Previously unreleased tracks from the 1977-'78 recording sessions include long-missed studio versions of such live standards as 'Because the Night', 'Fire' and Springsteen's most celebrated outtake, 'The Promise'. Finished in some cases with modern vocals and additional instrumentation, they form a 'lost album' between 'Born to Run' and 'Darkness'.

The Promise: The Making of Darkness on the Edge of Town
Released May 2011

This single-disc release of the Thom Zimny-directed documentary 'The Promise' breaks his story of the 'Darkness' album sessions out of the larger box set. Zimny's 'Songs from the Promise' is a major bonus feature: five songs from the E Street Band's 2010 Carousel House show in Asbury Park, which was Clarence Clemons' last appearance with the band.

MusiCares Person Of the Year: A Tribute to Bruce Springsteen
Released March 2014

On February 8 2013, Bruce Springsteen was honoured as the 2013 MusiCares Person Of The Year. MusiCares was established in 1989 by the Recording Academy to provide a safety net of critical assistance for music people in times of need, through innovative programs and services. A highlight of Grammy week activities, this recording brings together a stellar list of other artists paying tribute to Bruce and his music performing many of the songs he wrote throughout his illustrious career, as well as Bruce himself and the E Street Band performing new songs and a few favourites. Performers include Alabama Shakes, Patti Smith, Natalie Maines, Ben Harper, Charlie Musselwhite, Ken Casey, Mavis Staples, Zac Brown, Mumford & Sons, Jackson Browne, Tom Morello, Emmylou Harris, Kenny Chesney, Elton John, Juanes, Tim McGraw, Faith Hill, Jim James, John Legend, Sting, and Neil Young & Crazy Horse.

American Beauty
Released April 2014

A four-song EP released on limited edition 12-inch vinyl on April 19, 2014. A digital download version was also released on April 22, 2014. The four songs that appeared on the EP are outtakes from Springsteen's 2014 studio album 'High Hopes'.

The Ties That Bind: The River Collection
Released December 2015

'The Ties That Bind: The River Collection', Is a comprehensive look at 'The River' era, the set contains 52 tracks on 4 CDs with a wealth of unreleased material, and 4 hours of never-before-seen video on 3 DVDs.

Chapter and Verse
Released September 2016

'Chapter and Verse' is the musical companion to Bruce Springsteen's autobiography 'Born to Run.' The album is a collection of 18 songs chosen by Springsteen that trace his musical history from its earliest days and tell a story that parallels the one in the book. 'Chapter and Verse' includes five previously unreleased tracks including two tracks from The Castiles, featuring a teenage Springsteen on guitar and vocals.

Springsteen On Broadway
Released December 2018

'Springsteen on Broadway' features the songs and stories from Tony Award winner Bruce Springsteen's historic 236-show run at Jujamcyn's Walter Kerr Theatre and consists of the complete audio from the companion Netflix film. Based on his worldwide best-selling autobiography 'Born to Run', 'Springsteen on Broadway' is a unique evening with Bruce, his guitar, a piano, and his very personal stories.

Western Stars – Songs from The Film
Released 2019

'Western Stars – Songs from The Film' is the soundtrack album to Bruce Springsteen's directorial debut. The album features each of the live performances captured in the film 'Western Stars.' Listeners will be able to hear the film versions of every song from Springsteen's 2019 studio album, as well as a new cover of Glen Campbell's 'Rhinestone Cowboy'. In the film and on the album, Springsteen performs each of the 14 songs with special guest Patti Scialfa, backed by a band and full orchestra.

The Legendary 1979 No Nukes Concerts
Released November 2021

'The Legendary 1979 No Nukes Concerts' from Bruce Springsteen and the E Street Band feature Bruce Springsteen and The E Street Band's entire thirteen-song setlist from the September 1979 MUSE (Musicians United for Safe Energy) benefit concerts at Madison Square Garden in New York City. The concert includes footage of 10 never-before-released performances.